# *Amateur Radio Service*

## *Part 97*

### Kent Hertz

*Amateur Radio Service, Part 97*

The author believes, to the best of his knowledge, that the information provide in this book is correct at the time of this writing.

DISCLAIMER AND/OR LEGAL NOTICES:

Care has been taken to confirm the accuracy of the information presented. However, the author and publisher are not responsible for errors or omissions or for any consequences from application of the information in this book and make no warranty, expressed or implied, with respect to the currency, completeness, or accuracy of the contents of the publication.

# Table of Contents

PART 97—AMATEUR RADIO SERVICE .................................................................1

Subpart A—General Provisions ......................................................................4

§97.1 Basis and purpose. ...............................................................................4

§97.3 Definitions. .........................................................................................5

§97.5 Station license required.......................................................................15

§97.7 Control operation required. .................................................................18

§97.9 Operator license grant.........................................................................19

§97.11 Stations aboard ships or aircraft. ......................................................20

§97.13 Restrictions on station location. ........................................................21

§97.15 Station antenna structures. ...............................................................24

§97.17 Application for new license grant. ......................................................25

§97.19 Application for a vanity call sign. .......................................................27

§97.21 Application for a modified or renewed license grant.............................31

§97.23 Mailing address.................................................................................34

§97.25 License term. ....................................................................................35

§97.27 FCC modification of station license grant............................................36

§97.29 Replacement license grant document. ................................................37

§97.31 Cancellation on account of the licensee's death. .................................38

Subpart B—Station Operation Standards .......................................................39

§97.101 General standards............................................................................39

§97.103 Station licensee responsibilities. ......................................................40

§97.105 Control operator duties.....................................................................41

§97.107 Reciprocal operating authority. ........................................................42

§97.109 Station control. ................................................................................44

§97.111 Authorized transmissions. ................................................................45

§97.113 Prohibited transmissions. .................................................................47

§97.115 Third party communications. .............................................................50

§97.117 International communications. ...........................................................52

§97.119 Station identification. ........................................................................53

§97.121 Restricted operation. ................................................................56

Subpart C—Special Operations ..........................................................57

§97.201 Auxiliary station. ...................................................................57

§97.203 Beacon station. .....................................................................58

§97.205 Repeater station. ...................................................................60

§97.207 Space station. ........................................................................62

§97.209 Earth station. .........................................................................66

§97.211 Space telecommand station. ................................................67

§97.213 Telecommand of an amateur station. ...................................68

§97.215 Telecommand of model craft. ..............................................69

§97.217 Telemetry. .............................................................................70

§97.219 Message forwarding system. .............................................71

§97.221 Automatically controlled digital station. ...........................72

Subpart D—Technical Standards ........................................................73

§97.301 Authorized frequency bands. ............................................73

§97.303 Frequency sharing requirements. .....................................82

§97.305 Authorized emission types. ................................................90

§97.307 Emission standards. ..............................................................95

§97.309 RTTY and data emission codes. .......................................100

§97.311 SS emission types. ...............................................................102

§97.313 Transmitter power standards. ...........................................103

§97.315 Certification of external RF power amplifiers. ..................106

§97.317 Standards for certification of external RF power amplifiers. ................107

Subpart E—Providing Emergency Communications .........................108

§97.401 Operation during a disaster. ...........................................108

§97.403 Safety of life and protection of property. .........................109

§97.405 Station in distress. ..............................................................110

§97.407 Radio amateur civil emergency service. ...........................111

Subpart F—Qualifying Examination Systems .................................113

# Amateur Radio Service, Part 97

§97.501 Qualifying for an amateur operator license............................................113

§97.503 Element standards. .................................................................................114

§97.505 Element credit. .......................................................................................115

§97.507 Preparing an examination. ....................................................................116

§97.509 Administering VE requirements...........................................................117

§97.511 Examinee conduct..................................................................................120

§97.513 VE session manager requirements. .....................................................120

§§97.515-97.517 [Reserved]..............................................................................120

§97.519 Coordinating examination sessions......................................................121

§97.521 VEC qualifications. ...............................................................................123

§97.523 Question pools. .....................................................................................124

§97.525 Accrediting VEs......................................................................................125

§97.527 Reimbursement for expenses. ...............................................................126

Appendix 1 to Part 97—Places Where the Amateur Service is Regulated by the FCC..............................................................................................................127

Appendix 2 to Part 97—VEC Regions..............................................................128

Reference:.............................................................................................................129

Title 47: Telecommunication

# PART 97—AMATEUR RADIO SERVICE

## Contents
### Subpart A—General Provisions

§97.1 Basis and purpose.
§97.3 Definitions.
§97.5 Station license required.
§97.7 Control operation required.
§97.9 Operator license grant.
§97.11 Stations aboard ships or aircraft.
§97.13 Restrictions on station location.
§97.15 Station antenna structures.
§97.17 Application for new license grant.
§97.19 Application for a vanity call sign.
§97.21 Application for a modified or renewed license grant.
§97.23 Mailing address.
§97.25 License term.
§97.27 FCC modification of station license grant.
§97.29 Replacement license grant document.
§97.31 Cancellation on account of the licensee's death.

### Subpart B—Station Operation Standards

§97.101 General standards.
§97.103 Station licensee responsibilities.
§97.105 Control operator duties.
§97.107 Reciprocal operating authority.
§97.109 Station control.
§97.111 Authorized transmissions.
§97.113 Prohibited transmissions.
§97.115 Third party communications.
§97.117 International communications.

§97.119 Station identification.
§97.121 Restricted operation.
**Subpart C—Special Operations**

§97.201 Auxiliary station.
§97.203 Beacon station.
§97.205 Repeater station.
§97.207 Space station.
§97.209 Earth station.
§97.211 Space telecommand station.
§97.213 Telecommand of an amateur station.
§97.215 Telecommand of model craft.
§97.217 Telemetry.
§97.219 Message forwarding system.
§97.221 Automatically controlled digital station.
**Subpart D—Technical Standards**

§97.301 Authorized frequency bands.
§97.303 Frequency sharing requirements.
§97.305 Authorized emission types.
§97.307 Emission standards.
§97.309 RTTY and data emission codes.
§97.311 SS emission types.
§97.313 Transmitter power standards.
§97.315 Certification of external RF power amplifiers.
§97.317 Standards for certification of external RF power amplifiers.
**Subpart E—Providing Emergency Communications**

§97.401 Operation during a disaster.
§97.403 Safety of life and protection of property.
§97.405 Station in distress.
§97.407 Radio amateur civil emergency service.
**Subpart F—Qualifying Examination Systems**

§97.501 Qualifying for an amateur operator license.
§97.503 Element standards.

§97.505 Element credit.
§97.507 Preparing an examination.
§97.509 Administering VE requirements.
§97.511 Examinee conduct.
§97.513 VE session manager requirements.
§§97.515-97.517 [Reserved]
§97.519 Coordinating examination sessions.
§97.521 VEC qualifications.
§97.523 Question pools.
§97.525 Accrediting VEs.
§97.527 Reimbursement for expenses.
Appendix 1 to Part 97—Places Where the Amateur Service is Regulated by the FCC
Appendix 2 to Part 97—VEC Regions

AUTHORITY: 48 Stat. 1066, 1082, as amended; 47 U.S.C. 154, 303. Interpret or apply 48 Stat. 1064-1068, 1081-1105, as amended; 47 U.S.C. 151-155, 301-609, unless otherwise noted.

SOURCE: 54 FR 25857, June 20, 1989, unless otherwise noted.

EDITORIAL NOTE: Nomenclature changes to part 97 appear at 63 FR 54077, Oct. 8, 1998.

## Subpart A—General Provisions

### §97.1 Basis and purpose.

The rules and regulations in this part are designed to provide an amateur radio service having a fundamental purpose as expressed in the following principles:

(a) Recognition and enhancement of the value of the amateur service to the public as a voluntary noncommercial communication service, particularly with respect to providing emergency communications.

(b) Continuation and extension of the amateur's proven ability to contribute to the advancement of the radio art.

(c) Encouragement and improvement of the amateur service through rules which provide for advancing skills in both the communication and technical phases of the art.

(d) Expansion of the existing reservoir within the amateur radio service of trained operators, technicians, and electronics experts.

(e) Continuation and extension of the amateur's unique ability to enhance international goodwill.

## §97.3 Definitions.

(a) The definitions of terms used in part 97 are:

(1) *Amateur operator.* A person named in an amateur operator/primary license station grant on the ULS consolidated licensee database to be the control operator of an amateur station.

(2) *Amateur radio services.* The amateur service, the amateur-satellite service and the radio amateur civil emergency service.

(4) *Amateur service.* A radio communication service for the purpose of self-training, intercommunication and technical investigations carried out by amateurs, that is, duly authorized persons interested in radio technique solely with a personal aim and without pecuniary interest.

(5) *Amateur station.* A station in an amateur radio service consisting of the apparatus necessary for carrying on radio communications.

(6) *Automatic control.* The use of devices and procedures for control of a station when it is transmitting so that compliance with the FCC Rules is achieved without the control operator being present at a control point.

(7) *Auxiliary station.* An amateur station, other than in a message forwarding system, that is transmitting communications point-to-point within a system of cooperating amateur stations.

(8) *Bandwidth.* The width of a frequency band outside of which the mean power of the transmitted signal is attenuated at least 26 dB below the mean power of the transmitted signal within the band.

(9) *Beacon.* An amateur station transmitting communications for the purposes of observation of propagation and reception or other related experimental activities.

(10) *Broadcasting.* Transmissions intended for reception by the general public, either direct or relayed.

(11) *Call sign system.* The method used to select a call sign for amateur station over-the-air identification purposes. The call sign systems are:

(i) *Sequential call sign system.* The call sign is selected by the FCC from an alphabetized list corresponding to the geographic region of the licensee's mailing address and operator class. The call sign is shown on the license. The FCC will issue public announcements detailing the procedures of the sequential call sign system.

(ii) *Vanity call sign system.* The call sign is selected by the FCC from a list of call signs requested by the licensee. The call sign is shown on the license. The FCC will issue public announcements detailing the procedures of the vanity call sign system.

(iii) *Special event call sign system.* The call sign is selected by the station licensee from a list of call signs shown on a common data base coordinated, maintained and disseminated by the amateur station special event call sign data base coordinators. The call sign must have the single letter prefix K, N or W, followed by a single numeral 0 through 9, followed by a single letter A through W or Y or Z (for example K1A). The special event call sign is substituted for the call sign shown on the station license grant while the station is transmitting. The FCC will issue public announcements detailing the procedures of the special event call sign system.

(12) *CEPT radio amateur license.* A license issued by a country belonging to the European Conference of Postal and Telecommunications Administrations (CEPT) that has adopted Recommendation T/R 61-01 (Nice 1985, Paris 1992, Nicosia 2003).

(13) *Control operator.* An amateur operator designated by the licensee of a station to be responsible for the transmissions from that station to assure compliance with the FCC Rules.

(14) *Control point.* The location at which the control operator function is performed.

(15) *CSCE.* Certificate of successful completion of an examination.

(16) *Earth station.* An amateur station located on, or within 50 km of, the Earth's surface intended for communications with space stations or with other Earth stations by means of one or more other objects in space.

(17) [Reserved]

(18) *External RF power amplifier.* A device capable of increasing power output when used in conjunction with, but not an integral part of, a transmitter.

(19) [Reserved]

(20) *FAA.* Federal Aviation Administration.

(21) *FCC.* Federal Communications Commission.

(22) *Frequency coordinator.* An entity, recognized in a local or regional area by amateur operators whose stations are eligible to be auxiliary or repeater stations, that

recommends transmit/receive channels and associated operating and technical parameters for such stations in order to avoid or minimize potential interference.

(23) *Harmful interference.* Interference which endangers the functioning of a radio navigation service or of other safety services or seriously degrades, obstructs or repeatedly interrupts a radio communication service operating in accordance with the Radio Regulations.

(24) *IARP (International Amateur Radio Permit).* A document issued pursuant to the terms of the Inter-American Convention on an International Amateur Radio Permit by a country signatory to that Convention, other than the United States. Montrouis, Haiti. AG/doc.3216/95.

(25) *Indicator.* Words, letters or numerals appended to and separated from the call sign during the station identification.

(26) *Information bulletin.* A message directed only to amateur operators consisting solely of subject matter of direct interest to the amateur service.

(27) *In-law.* A parent, stepparent, sibling, or step-sibling of a licensee's spouse; the spouse of a licensee's sibling, step-sibling, child, or stepchild; or the spouse of a licensee's spouse's sibling or step-sibling.

(28) *International Morse code.* A dot-dash code as defined in ITU-T Recommendation F.1 (March, 1998), Division B, I. Morse code.

(29) *ITU.* International Telecommunication Union.

(30) *Line A.* Begins at Aberdeen, WA, running by great circle arc to the intersection of 48° N, 120° W, thence

along parallel 48° N, to the intersection of 95° W, thence by great circle arc through the southernmost point of Duluth, MN, thence by great circle arc to 45° N, 85° W, thence southward along meridian 85° W, to its intersection with parallel 41° N, thence along parallel 41° N, to its intersection with meridian 82° W, thence by great circle arc through the southernmost point of Bangor, ME, thence by great circle arc through the southernmost point of Searsport, ME, at which point it terminates.

(31) *Local control.* The use of a control operator who directly manipulates the operating adjustments in the station to achieve compliance with the FCC Rules.

(32) *Message forwarding system.* A group of amateur stations participating in a voluntary, cooperative, interactive arrangement where communications are sent from the control operator of an originating station to the control operator of one or more destination stations by one or more forwarding stations.

(33) *National Radio Quiet Zone.* The area in Maryland, Virginia and West Virginia Bounded by 39°15′ N on the north, 78°30′ W on the east, 37°30′ N on the south and 80°30′ W on the west.

(34) *Physician.* For the purpose of this part, a person who is licensed to practice in a place where the amateur service is regulated by the FCC, as either a Doctor of Medicine (M.D.) or a Doctor of Osteopathy (D.O.)

(35) *Question pool.* All current examination questions for a designated written examination element.

(36) *Question set.* A series of examination questions on a given examination selected from the question pool.

(37) *Radio Regulations.* The latest ITU *Radio Regulations* to which the United States is a party.

(38) *RACES* (radio amateur civil emergency service). A radio service using amateur stations for civil defense communications during periods of local, regional or national civil emergencies.

(39) *Remote control.* The use of a control operator who indirectly manipulates the operating adjustments in the station through a control link to achieve compliance with the FCC Rules.

(40) *Repeater.* An amateur station that simultaneously retransmits the transmission of another amateur station on a different channel or channels.

(41) *Space station.* An amateur station located more than 50 km above the Earth's surface.

(42) *Space telemetry.* A one-way transmission from a space station of measurements made from the measuring instruments in a spacecraft, including those relating to the functioning of the spacecraft.

(43) *Spurious emission.* An emission, or frequencies outside the necessary bandwidth of a transmission, the level of which may be reduced without affecting the information being transmitted.

(44) *Telecommand.* A one-way transmission to initiate, modify, or terminate functions of a device at a distance.

(45) *Telecommand station.* An amateur station that transmits communications to initiate, modify or terminate functions of a space station.

(46) *Telemetry.* A one-way transmission of measurements at a distance from the measuring instrument.

(47) *Third party communications.* A message from the control operator (first party) of an amateur station to another amateur station control operator (second party) on behalf of another person (third party).

(48) *ULS (Universal Licensing System).* The consolidated database, application filing system and processing system for all Wireless Telecommunications Services.

(49) *VE.* Volunteer examiner.

(50) *VEC.* Volunteer-examiner coordinator.

(b) The definitions of technical symbols used in this part are:

(1) *EHF* (extremely high frequency). The frequency range 30-300 GHz.

(2) *HF* (high frequency). The frequency range 3-30 MHz.

(3) *Hz.* Hertz.

(4) *m.* Meters.

(5) *MF* (medium frequency). The frequency range 300-3000 kHz.

(6) *PEP* (peak envelope power). The average power supplied to the antenna transmission line by a transmitter

during one RF cycle at the crest of the modulation envelope taken under normal operating conditions.

(7) *RF.* Radio frequency.

(8) *SHF* (super-high frequency). The frequency range 3-30 GHz.

(9) *UHF* (ultra-high frequency). The frequency range 300-3000 MHz.

(10) *VHF* (very-high frequency). The frequency range 30-300 MHz.

(11) *W.* Watts.

(c) The following terms are used in this part to indicate emission types. Refer to §2.201 of the FCC Rules, *Emission, modulation and transmission characteristics,* for information on emission type designators.

(1) *CW.* International Morse code telegraphy emissions having designators with A, C, H, J or R as the first symbol; 1 as the second symbol; A or B as the third symbol; and emissions J2A and J2B.

(2) *Data.* Telemetry, telecommand and computer communications emissions having (i) designators with A, C, D, F, G, H, J or R as the first symbol, 1 as the second symbol, and D as the third symbol; (ii) emission J2D; and (iii) emissions A1C, F1C, F2C, J2C, and J3C having an occupied bandwidth of 500 Hz or less when transmitted on an amateur service frequency below 30 MHz. Only a digital code of a type specifically authorized in this part may be transmitted.

(3) *Image.* Facsimile and television emissions having designators with A, C, D, F, G, H, J or R as the first symbol; 1, 2 or 3 as the second symbol; C or F as the third symbol; and emissions having B as the first symbol; 7, 8 or 9 as the second symbol; W as the third symbol.

(4) *MCW.* Tone-modulated international Morse code telegraphy emissions having designators with A, C, D, F, G, H or R as the first symbol; 2 as the second symbol; A or B as the third symbol.

(5) *Phone.* Speech and other sound emissions having designators with A, C, D, F, G, H, J or R as the first symbol; 1, 2 or 3 as the second symbol; E as the third symbol. Also speech emissions having B as the first symbol; 7, 8 or 9 as the second symbol; E as the third symbol. MCW for the purpose of performing the station identification procedure, or for providing telegraphy practice interspersed with speech. Incidental tones for the purpose of selective calling or alerting or to control the level of a demodulated signal may also be considered phone.

(6) *Pulse.* Emissions having designators with K, L, M, P, Q, V or W as the first symbol; 0, 1, 2, 3, 7, 8, 9 or X as the second symbol; A, B, C, D, E, F, N, W or X as the third symbol.

(7) *RTTY.* Narrow-band direct-printing telegraphy emissions having designators with A, C, D, F, G, H, J or R as the first symbol; 1 as the second symbol; B as the third symbol; and emission J2B. Only a digital code of a type specifically authorized in this part may be transmitted.

(8) *SS.* Spread spectrum emissions using bandwidth-expansion modulation emissions having designators with

A, C, D, F, G, H, J or R as the first symbol; X as the second symbol; X as the third symbol.

(9) *Test.* Emissions containing no information having the designators with N as the third symbol. Test does not include pulse emissions with no information or modulation unless pulse emissions are also authorized in the frequency band.

[54 FR 25857, June 20, 1989]

EDITORIAL NOTE: For FEDERAL REGISTER citations affecting §97.3, see the List of CFR Sections Affected, which appears in the Finding Aids section of the printed volume and at *www.fdsys.gov.*

## §97.5 Station license required.

(a) The station apparatus must be under the physical control of a person named in an amateur station license grant on the ULS consolidated license database or a person authorized for alien reciprocal operation by §97.107 of this part, before the station may transmit on any amateur service frequency from any place that is:

(1) Within 50 km of the Earth's surface and at a place where the amateur service is regulated by the FCC;

(2) Within 50 km of the Earth's surface and aboard any vessel or craft that is documented or registered in the United States; or

(3) More than 50 km above the Earth's surface aboard any craft that is documented or registered in the United States.

(b) The types of station license grants are:

(1) *An operator/primary station license grant.* One, but only one, operator/primary station license grant may be held by any one person. The primary station license is granted together with the amateur operator license. Except for a representative of a foreign government, any person who qualifies by examination is eligible to apply for an operator/primary station license grant.

(2) *A club station license grant.* A club station license grant may be held only by the person who is the license trustee designated by an officer of the club. The trustee must be a person who holds an operator/primary station license grant. The club must be composed of at least four persons and must have a name, a document of organization, management, and a primary purpose

devoted to amateur service activities consistent with this part.

(3) *A military recreation station license grant.* A military recreation station license grant may be held only by the person who is the license custodian designated by the official in charge of the United States military recreational premises where the station is situated. The person must not be a representative of a foreign government. The person need not hold an amateur operator license grant.

(c) The person named in the station license grant or who is authorized for alien reciprocal operation by §97.107 of this part may use, in accordance with the applicable rules of this part, the transmitting apparatus under the physical control of the person at places where the amateur service is regulated by the FCC.

(d) A CEPT radio-amateur license is issued to the person by the country of which the person is a citizen. The person must not:

(1) Be a resident alien or citizen of the United States, regardless of any other citizenship also held;

(2) Hold an FCC-issued amateur operator license nor reciprocal permit for alien amateur licensee;

(3) Be a prior amateur service licensee whose FCC-issued license was revoked, suspended for less than the balance of the license term and the suspension is still in effect, suspended for the balance of the license term and relicensing has not taken place, or surrendered for cancellation following notice of revocation, suspension or monetary forfeiture proceedings; or

(4) Be the subject of a cease and desist order that relates to amateur service operation and which is still in effect.

(e) An IARP is issued to the person by the country of which the person is a citizen. The person must not:

(1) Be a resident alien or citizen of the United States, regardless of any other citizenship also held;

(2) Hold an FCC-issued amateur operator license nor reciprocal permit for alien amateur licensee;

(3) Be a prior amateur service licensee whose FCC-issued license was revoked, suspended for less than the balance of the license term and the suspension is still in effect, suspended for the balance of the license term and relicensing has not taken place, or surrendered for cancellation following notice of revocation, suspension or monetary forfeiture proceedings; or

(4) Be the subject of a cease and desist order that relates to amateur service operation and which is still in effect.

[59 FR 54831, Nov. 2, 1994, as amended at 62 FR 17567, Apr. 10, 1997; 63 FR 68977, Dec. 14, 1998; 75 FR 78169, Dec. 15, 2010]

**§97.7 Control operation required.**

When transmitting, each amateur station must have a control operator. The control operator must be a person:

(a) For whom an amateur operator/primary station license grant appears on the ULS consolidated licensee database, or

(b) Who is authorized for alien reciprocal operation by §97.107 of this part.

[63 FR 68978, Dec. 14, 1998]

## §97.9 Operator license grant.

(a) The classes of amateur operator license grants are: Novice, Technician, General, Advanced, and Amateur Extra. The person named in the operator license grant is authorized to be the control operator of an amateur station with the privileges authorized to the operator class specified on the license grant.

(b) The person named in an operator license grant of Novice, Technician, General or Advanced Class, who has properly submitted to the administering VEs a FCC Form 605 document requesting examination for an operator license grant of a higher class, and who holds a CSCE indicating that the person has completed the necessary examinations within the previous 365 days, is authorized to exercise the rights and privileges of the higher operator class until final disposition of the application or until 365 days following the passing of the examination, whichever comes first.

[75 FR 78169, Dec. 15, 2010]

## §97.11 Stations aboard ships or aircraft.

(a) The installation and operation of an amateur station on a ship or aircraft must be approved by the master of the ship or pilot in command of the aircraft.

(b) The station must be separate from and independent of all other radio apparatus installed on the ship or aircraft, except a common antenna may be shared with a voluntary ship radio installation. The station's transmissions must not cause interference to any other apparatus installed on the ship or aircraft.

(c) The station must not constitute a hazard to the safety of life or property. For a station aboard an aircraft, the apparatus shall not be operated while the aircraft is operating under Instrument Flight Rules, as defined by the FAA, unless the station has been found to comply with all applicable FAA Rules.

## §97.13 Restrictions on station location.

(a) Before placing an amateur station on land of environmental importance or that is significant in American history, architecture or culture, the licensee may be required to take certain actions prescribed by §§1.1305-1.1319 of this chapter.

(b) A station within 1600 m (1 mile) of an FCC monitoring facility must protect that facility from harmful interference. Failure to do so could result in imposition of operating restrictions upon the amateur station by a District Director pursuant to §97.121 of this part. Geographical coordinates of the facilities that require protection are listed in §0.121(c) of this chapter.

(c) Before causing or allowing an amateur station to transmit from any place where the operation of the station could cause human exposure to RF electromagnetic field levels in excess of those allowed under §1.1310 of this chapter, the licensee is required to take certain actions.

(1) The licensee must perform the routine RF environmental evaluation prescribed by §1.1307(b) of this chapter, if the power of the licensee's station exceeds the limits given in the following table:

*Amateur Radio Service, Part 97*

| Wavelength band | Evaluation required if power[1] (watts) exceeds |
|---|---|
| **MF** | |
| 160 m | 500 |
| **HF** | |
| 80 m | 500 |
| 75 m | 500 |
| 40 m | 500 |
| 30 m | 425 |
| 20 m | 225 |
| 17 m | 125 |
| 15 m | 100 |
| 12 m | 75 |
| 10 m | 50 |
| VHF (all bands) | 50 |
| **UHF** | |
| 70 cm | 70 |
| 33 cm | 150 |
| 23 cm | 200 |
| 13 cm | 250 |
| SHF (all bands) | 250 |
| EHF (all bands) | 250 |
| Repeater stations (all bands) | *non-building-mounted antennas:* height above ground level to lowest point of antenna <10 m *and* power >500 W ERP *building-mounted antennas:* power >500 W ERP |

[1]Power = PEP input to antenna except, for repeater stations only, power exclusion is based on ERP (effective radiated power).

(2) If the routine environmental evaluation indicates that the RF electromagnetic fields could exceed the limits contained in §1.1310 of this chapter in accessible areas, the licensee must take action to prevent human exposure to such RF electromagnetic fields. Further information on evaluating compliance with these limits can be found in the FCC's OET Bulletin Number 65, "Evaluating Compliance with FCC Guidelines for Human Exposure to Radiofrequency Electromagnetic Fields."

[54 FR 25857, June 20, 1989, as amended at 55 FR 20398, May 16, 1990; 61 FR 41019, Aug. 7, 1996; 62 FR 47963, Sept. 12, 1997; 62 FR 49557, Sept. 22, 1997; 62 FR 61448, Nov. 18, 1997; 63 FR 68978, Dec. 14, 1998; 65 FR 6549, Feb. 10, 2000]

**§97.15 Station antenna structures.**

(a) Owners of certain antenna structures more than 60.96 meters (200 feet) above ground level at the site or located near or at a public use airport must notify the Federal Aviation Administration and register with the Commission as required by part 17 of this chapter.

(b) Except as otherwise provided herein, a station antenna structure may be erected at heights and dimensions sufficient to accommodate amateur service communications. (State and local regulation of a station antenna structure must not preclude amateur service communications. Rather, it must reasonably accommodate such communications and must constitute the minimum practicable regulation to accomplish the state or local authority's legitimate purpose. *See* PRB-1, 101 FCC 2d 952 (1985) for details.)

[64 FR 53242, Oct. 1, 1999]

## §97.17 Application for new license grant.

(a) Any qualified person is eligible to apply for a new operator/primary station, club station or military recreation station license grant. No new license grant will be issued for a Novice or Advanced Class operator/primary station.

(b) Each application for a new amateur service license grant must be filed with the FCC as follows:

(1) Each candidate for an amateur radio operator license which requires the applicant to pass one or more examination elements must present the administering VEs with all information required by the rules prior to the examination. The VEs may collect all necessary information in any manner of their choosing, including creating their own forms.

(2) For a new club or military recreation station license grant, each applicant must present all information required by the rules to an amateur radio organization having tax-exempt status under section 501(c)(3) of the Internal Revenue Code of 1986 that provides voluntary, uncompensated and unreimbursed services in providing club and military recreation station call signs ("*Club Station Call Sign Administrator*") who must submit the information to the FCC in an electronic batch file. The Club Station Call Sign Administrator may collect the information required by these rules in any manner of their choosing, including creating their own forms. The Club Station Call Sign Administrator must retain the applicants information for at least 15 months and make it available to the FCC upon request. The FCC will issue public announcements listing the qualified organizations that have completed a pilot autogrant batch filing project and are authorized to serve as a Club Station Call Sign Administrator.

(c) No person shall obtain or attempt to obtain, or assist another person to obtain or attempt to obtain, an amateur service license grant by fraudulent means.

(d) One unique call sign will be shown on the license grant of each new primary, club and military recreation station. The call sign will be selected by the sequential call sign system. Effective February 14, 2011, no club station license grants will be issued to a licensee who is shown as the license trustee on an existing club station license grant.

[63 FR 68978, Dec. 14, 1998. as amended at 64 FR 53242, Oct. 1, 1999; 65 FR 6549, Feb. 10, 2000; 75 FR 78170, Dec. 15, 2010]

## §97.19 Application for a vanity call sign.

(a) The person named in an operator/primary station license grant or in a club station license grant is eligible to make application for modification of the license grant, or the renewal thereof, to show a call sign selected by the vanity call sign system. Effective February 14, 2011, the person named in a club station license grant that shows on the license a call sign that was selected by a trustee is not eligible for an additional vanity call sign. (The person named in a club station license grant that shows on the license a call sign that was selected by a trustee is eligible for a vanity call sign for his or her operator/primary station license grant on the same basis as any other person who holds an operator/primary station license grant.) Military recreation stations are not eligible for a vanity call sign.

(b) Each application for a modification of an operator/primary or club station license grant, or the renewal thereof, to show a call sign selected by the vanity call sign system must be filed in accordance with §1.913 of this chapter.

(c) Unassigned call signs are available to the vanity call sign system with the following exceptions:

(1) A call sign shown on an expired license grant is not available to the vanity call sign system for 2 years following the expiration of the license.

(2) A call sign shown on a surrendered or canceled license grant (except for a license grant that is canceled pursuant to §97.31) is not available to the vanity call sign system for 2 years following the date such action is taken. (The availability of a call sign shown on a license canceled pursuant to §97.31 is governed by paragraph (c)(3) of this section.)

(i) This 2-year period does not apply to any license grant pursuant to paragraph (c)(3)(i), (ii), or (iii) of this section that is surrendered, canceled, revoked, voided, or set aside because the grantee acknowledged or the Commission determined that the grantee was not eligible for the exception. In such a case, the call sign is not available to the vanity call sign system for 30 days following the date such action is taken, or for the period for which the call sign would not have been available to the vanity call sign system pursuant to paragraphs (c)(2) or (3) of this section but for the intervening grant to the ineligible applicant, whichever is later.

(ii) An applicant to whose operator/primary station license grant, or club station license grant for which the applicant is the trustee, the call sign was previously assigned is exempt from the 2-year period set forth in paragraph (c)(2) of this section.

(3) A call sign shown on a license canceled pursuant to §97.31 of this part is not available to the vanity call sign system for 2 years following the person's death, or for 2 years following the expiration of the license grant, whichever is sooner. If, however, a license is canceled more than 2 years after the licensee's death (or within 30 days before the second anniversary of the licensee's death), the call sign is not available to the vanity call sign system for 30 days following the date such action is taken. The following applicants are exempt from this 2-year period:

(i) An applicant to whose operator/primary station license grant, or club station license grant for which the applicant is the trustee, the call sign was previously assigned; or

(ii) An applicant who is the spouse, child, grandchild, stepchild, parent, grandparent, stepparent, brother, sister, stepbrother, stepsister, aunt, uncle, niece, nephew, or in-law of the person now deceased or of any other deceased former holder of the call sign, provided that the vanity call sign requested by the applicant is from the group of call signs corresponding to the same or lower class of operator license held by the applicant as designated in the sequential call sign system; or

(iii) An applicant who is a club station license trustee acting with a written statement of consent signed by either the licensee *ante mortem* but who is now deceased, or by at least one relative as listed in paragraph (c)(3)(ii) of this section, of the person now deceased or of any other deceased former holder of the call sign, provided that the deceased former holder was a member of the club during his or her life.

(d) The vanity call sign requested by an applicant must be selected from the group of call signs corresponding to the same or lower class of operator license held by the applicant as designated in the sequential call sign system.

(1) The applicant must request that the call sign shown on the license grant be vacated and provide a list of up to 25 call signs in order of preference. In the event that the Commission receives more than one application requesting a vanity call sign from an applicant on the same receipt day, the Commission will process only the first such application entered into the Universal Licensing System. Subsequent vanity call sign applications from that applicant with the same receipt date will not be accepted.

(2) The first assignable call sign from the applicant's list will be shown on the license grant. When none of those

call signs are assignable, the call sign vacated by the applicant will be shown on the license grant.

(3) Vanity call signs will be selected from those call signs assignable at the time the application is processed by the FCC.

(4) A call sign designated under the sequential call sign system for Alaska, Hawaii, Caribbean Insular Areas, and Pacific Insular areas will be assigned only to a primary or club station whose licensee's mailing address is in the corresponding state, commonwealth, or island. This limitation does not apply to an applicant for the call sign as the spouse, child, grandchild, stepchild, parent, grandparent, stepparent, brother, sister, stepbrother, stepsister, aunt, uncle, niece, nephew, or in-law, of the former holder now deceased.

[60 FR 7460, Feb. 8, 1995, as amended at 60 FR 50123, Sept. 28, 1995; 60 FR 53132, Oct. 12, 1995; 63 FR 68979, Dec. 14, 1998; 71 FR 66461, Nov. 15, 2006; 75 FR 78170, Dec. 15, 2010]

## §97.21 Application for a modified or renewed license grant.

(a) A person holding a valid amateur station license grant:

(1) Must apply to the FCC for a modification of the license grant as necessary to show the correct mailing address, licensee name, club name, license trustee name, or license custodian name in accordance with §1.913 of this chapter. For a club or military recreation station license grant, the application must be presented in document form to a Club Station Call Sign Administrator who must submit the information thereon to the FCC in an electronic batch file. The Club Station Call Sign Administrator must retain the collected information for at least 15 months and make it available to the FCC upon request. A Club Station Call Sign Administrator shall not file with the Commission any application to modify a club station license grant that was submitted by a person other than the trustee as shown on the license grant, except an application to change the club station license trustee. An application to modify a club station license grant to change the license trustee name must be submitted to a Club Station Call Sign Administrator and must be signed by an officer of the club.

(2) May apply to the FCC for a modification of the operator/primary station license grant to show a higher operator class. Applicants must present the administering VEs with all information required by the rules prior to the examination. The VEs may collect all necessary information in any manner of their choosing, including creating their own forms.

(3) May apply to the FCC for renewal of the license grant for another term in accordance with §§1.913 and 1.949 of this chapter. Application for renewal of a

Technician Plus Class operator/primary station license will be processed as an application for renewal of a Technician Class operator/primary station license.

(i) For a station license grant showing a call sign obtained through the vanity call sign system, the application must be filed in accordance with §97.19 of this part in order to have the vanity call sign reassigned to the station.

(ii) For a primary station license grant showing a call sign obtained through the sequential call sign system, and for a primary station license grant showing a call sign obtained through the vanity call sign system but whose grantee does not want to have the vanity call sign reassigned to the station, the application must be filed with the FCC in accordance with §1.913 of this chapter. When the application has been received by the FCC on or before the license expiration date, the license operating authority is continued until the final disposition of the application.

(iii) For a club station or military recreation station license grant showing a call sign obtained through the sequential call sign system, and for a club station license grant showing a call sign obtained through the vanity call sign system but whose grantee does not want to have the vanity call sign reassigned to the station, the application must be presented in document form to a Club Station Call Sign Administrator who must submit the information thereon to the FCC in an electronic batch file. The replacement call sign will be selected by the sequential call sign system. The Club Station Call Sign Administrator must retain the collected information for at least 15 months and make it available to the FCC upon request.

(b) A person whose amateur station license grant has expired may apply to the FCC for renewal of the license grant for another term during a 2 year filing grace period. The application must be received at the address specified above prior to the end of the grace period. Unless and until the license grant is renewed, no privileges in this part are conferred.

(c) Except as provided in paragraph (a)(4) of this section, a call sign obtained under the sequential or vanity call sign system will be reassigned to the station upon renewal or modification of a station license.

[63 FR 68979, Dec. 14, 1998, as amended at 64 FR 53242, Oct. 1, 1999; 65 FR 6550, Feb. 10, 2000; 75 FR 78170, Dec. 15, 2010]

## 97.23 Mailing address.

Each license grant must show the grantee's correct name and mailing address. The mailing address must be in an area where the amateur service is regulated by the FCC and where the grantee can receive mail delivery by the United States Postal Service. Revocation of the station license or suspension of the operator license may result when correspondence from the FCC is returned as undeliverable because the grantee failed to provide the correct mailing address.

[63 FR 68979, Dec. 14, 1998]

## §97.25 License term.

An amateur service license is normally granted for a 10-year term.

[63 FR 68979, Dec. 14, 1998]

## §97.27 FCC modification of station license grant.

(a) The FCC may modify a station license grant, either for a limited time or for the duration of the term thereof, if it determines:

(1) That such action will promote the public interest, convenience, and necessity; or

(2) That such action will promote fuller compliance with the provisions of the Communications Act of 1934, as amended, or of any treaty ratified by the United States.

(b) When the FCC makes such a determination, it will issue an order of modification. The order will not become final until the licensee is notified in writing of the proposed action and the grounds and reasons therefor. The licensee will be given reasonable opportunity of no less than 30 days to protest the modification; except that, where safety of life or property is involved, a shorter period of notice may be provided. Any protest by a licensee of an FCC order of modification will be handled in accordance with the provisions of 47 U.S.C. 316.

[59 FR 54833, Nov. 2, 1994, as amended at 63 FR 68979, Dec. 14, 1998]

## §97.29 Replacement license grant document.

Each grantee whose amateur station license grant document is lost, mutilated or destroyed may apply to the FCC for a replacement in accordance with §1.913 of this chapter.

[63 FR 68979, Dec. 14, 1998]

## §97.31 Cancellation on account of the licensee's death.

(a) A person may request cancellation of an operator/primary station license grant on account of the licensee's death by submitting a signed request that includes a death certificate, obituary, or Social Security Death Index data that shows the person named in the operator/primary station license grant has died. Such a request may be submitted as a pleading associated with the deceased licensee's license. *See* §1.45 of this chapter. In addition, the Commission may cancel an operator/primary station license grant if it becomes aware of the grantee's death through other means. No action will be taken during the last thirty days of the post-expiration grace period (*see* §97.21(b)) on a request to cancel a license due to the licensee's death.

(b) A license that is canceled due to the licensee's death is canceled as of the date of the licensee's death.

[75 FR 78171, Dec. 15, 2010]

# Subpart B—Station Operation Standards

### §97.101 General standards.

(a) In all respects not specifically covered by FCC Rules each amateur station must be operated in accordance with good engineering and good amateur practice.

(b) Each station licensee and each control operator must cooperate in selecting transmitting channels and in making the most effective use of the amateur service frequencies. No frequency will be assigned for the exclusive use of any station.

(c) At all times and on all frequencies, each control operator must give priority to stations providing emergency communications, except to stations transmitting communications for training drills and tests in RACES.

(d) No amateur operator shall willfully or maliciously interfere with or cause interference to any radio communication or signal.

**§97.103 Station licensee responsibilities.**

(a) The station licensee is responsible for the proper operation of the station in accordance with the FCC Rules. When the control operator is a different amateur operator than the station licensee, both persons are equally responsible for proper operation of the station.

(b) The station licensee must designate the station control operator. The FCC will presume that the station licensee is also the control operator, unless documentation to the contrary is in the station records.

(c) The station licensee must make the station and the station records available for inspection upon request by an FCC representative.

[54 FR 25857, June 20, 1989, as amended at 71 FR 66462, Nov. 15, 2006; 75 FR 27201, May 14, 2010]

## §97.105 Control operator duties.

(a) The control operator must ensure the immediate proper operation of the station, regardless of the type of control.

(b) A station may only be operated in the manner and to the extent permitted by the privileges authorized for the class of operator license held by the control operator.

## §97.107 Reciprocal operating authority.

A non-citizen of the United States ("alien") holding an amateur service authorization granted by the alien's government is authorized to be the control operator of an amateur station located at places where the amateur service is regulated by the FCC, provided there is in effect a multilateral or bilateral reciprocal operating arrangement, to which the United States and the alien's government are parties, for amateur service operation on a reciprocal basis. The FCC will issue public announcements listing the countries with which the United States has such an arrangement. No citizen of the United States or person holding an FCC amateur operator/primary station license grant is eligible for the reciprocal operating authority granted by this section. The privileges granted to a control operator under this authorization are:

(a) For an amateur service license granted by the Government of Canada:

(1) The terms of the *Convention Between the United States and Canada* (TIAS No. 2508) *Relating to the Operation by Citizens of Either Country of Certain Radio Equipment or Stations in the Other Country;*

(2) The operating terms and conditions of the amateur service license issued by the Government of Canada; and

(3) The applicable rules of this part, but not to exceed the control operator privileges of an FCC-granted Amateur Extra Class operator license.

(b) For an amateur service license granted by any country, other than Canada, with which the United States has a multilateral or bilateral agreement:

(1) The terms of the agreement between the alien's government and the United States;

(2) The operating terms and conditions of the amateur service license granted by the alien's government;

(3) The applicable rules of this part, but not to exceed the control operator privileges of an FCC-granted Amateur Extra Class operator license; and

(c) At any time the FCC may, in its discretion, modify, suspend or cancel the reciprocal operating authority granted to any person by this section.

[63 FR 68979, Dec. 14, 1998]

## §97.109 Station control.

(a) Each amateur station must have at least one control point.

(b) When a station is being locally controlled, the control operator must be at the control point. Any station may be locally controlled.

(c) When a station is being remotely controlled, the control operator must be at the control point. Any station may be remotely controlled.

(d) When a station is being automatically controlled, the control operator need not be at the control point. Only stations specifically designated elsewhere in this part may be automatically controlled. Automatic control must cease upon notification by a District Director that the station is transmitting improperly or causing harmful interference to other stations. Automatic control must not be resumed without prior approval of the District Director.

[54 FR 39535, Sept. 27, 1989, as amended at 60 FR 26001, May 16, 1995; 69 FR 24997, May 5, 2004]

## §97.111 Authorized transmissions.

(a) An amateur station may transmit the following types of two-way communications:

(1) Transmissions necessary to exchange messages with other stations in the amateur service, except those in any country whose administration has notified the ITU that it objects to such communications. The FCC will issue public notices of current arrangements for international communications.

(2) Transmissions necessary to meet essential communication needs and to facilitate relief actions.

(3) Transmissions necessary to exchange messages with a station in another FCC-regulated service while providing emergency communications;

(4) Transmissions necessary to exchange messages with a United States government station, necessary to providing communications in RACES; and

(5) Transmissions necessary to exchange messages with a station in a service not regulated by the FCC, but authorized by the FCC to communicate with amateur stations. An amateur station may exchange messages with a participating United States military station during an Armed Forces Day Communications Test.

(b) In addition to one-way transmissions specifically authorized elsewhere in this part, an amateur station may transmit the following types of one-way communications:

(1) Brief transmissions necessary to make adjustments to the station;

(2) Brief transmissions necessary to establishing two-way communications with other stations;

(3) Telecommand;

(4) Transmissions necessary to providing emergency communications;

(5) Transmissions necessary to assisting persons learning, or improving proficiency in, the international Morse code; and

(6) Transmissions necessary to disseminate information bulletins.

(7) Transmissions of telemetry.

[54 FR 25857, June 20, 1989, as amended at 56 FR 56171, Nov. 1, 1991; 71 FR 25982, May 3, 2006; 71 FR 66462, Nov. 15, 2006]

## §97.113 Prohibited transmissions.

(a) No amateur station shall transmit:

(1) Communications specifically prohibited elsewhere in this part;

(2) Communications for hire or for material compensation, direct or indirect, paid or promised, except as otherwise provided in these rules;

(3) Communications in which the station licensee or control operator has a pecuniary interest, including communications on behalf of an employer, with the following exceptions:

(i) A station licensee or control station operator may participate on behalf of an employer in an emergency preparedness or disaster readiness test or drill, limited to the duration and scope of such test or drill, and operational testing immediately prior to such test or drill. Tests or drills that are not government-sponsored are limited to a total time of one hour per week; except that no more than twice in any calendar year, they may be conducted for a period not to exceed 72 hours.

(ii) An amateur operator may notify other amateur operators of the availability for sale or trade of apparatus normally used in an amateur station, provided that such activity is not conducted on a regular basis.

(iii) A control operator may accept compensation as an incident of a teaching position during periods of time when an amateur station is used by that teacher as a part of classroom instruction at an educational institution.

(iv) The control operator of a club station may accept compensation for the periods of time when the station is transmitting telegraphy practice or information bulletins, provided that the station transmits such telegraphy practice and bulletins for at least 40 hours per week; schedules operations on at least six amateur service MF and HF bands using reasonable measures to maximize coverage; where the schedule of normal operating times and frequencies is published at least 30 days in advance of the actual transmissions; and where the control operator does not accept any direct or indirect compensation for any other service as a control operator.

(4) Music using a phone emission except as specifically provided elsewhere in this section; communications intended to facilitate a criminal act; messages encoded for the purpose of obscuring their meaning, except as otherwise provided herein; obscene or indecent words or language; or false or deceptive messages, signals or identification.

(5) Communications, on a regular basis, which could reasonably be furnished alternatively through other radio services.

(b) An amateur station shall not engage in any form of broadcasting, nor may an amateur station transmit one-way communications except as specifically provided in these rules; nor shall an amateur station engage in any activity related to program production or news gathering for broadcasting purposes, except that communications directly related to the immediate safety of human life or the protection of property may be provided by amateur stations to broadcasters for dissemination to the public where no other means of communication is reasonably available before or at the time of the event.

(c) No station shall retransmit programs or signals emanating from any type of radio station other than an amateur station, except propagation and weather forecast information intended for use by the general public and originated from United States Government stations, and communications, including incidental music, originating on United States Government frequencies between a manned spacecraft and its associated Earth stations. Prior approval for manned spacecraft communications retransmissions must be obtained from the National Aeronautics and Space Administration. Such retransmissions must be for the exclusive use of amateur radio operators. Propagation, weather forecasts, and manned spacecraft communications retransmissions may not be conducted on a regular basis, but only occasionally, as an incident of normal amateur radio communications.

(d) No amateur station, except an auxiliary, repeater, or space station, may automatically retransmit the radio signals of other amateur station.

[58 FR 43072, Aug. 13, 1993; 58 FR 47219, Sept. 8, 1993, as amended at 71 FR 25982, May 3, 2006; 71 FR 66462, Nov. 15, 2006; 75 FR 46857, Aug. 4, 2010]

## §97.115 Third party communications.

(a) An amateur station may transmit messages for a third party to:

(1) Any station within the jurisdiction of the United States.

(2) Any station within the jurisdiction of any foreign government when transmitting emergency or disaster relief communications and any station within the jurisdiction of any foreign government whose administration has made arrangements with the United States to allow amateur stations to be used for transmitting international communications on behalf of third parties. No station shall transmit messages for a third party to any station within the jurisdiction of any foreign government whose administration has not made such an arrangement. This prohibition does not apply to a message for any third party who is eligible to be a control operator of the station.

(b) The third party may participate in stating the message where:

(1) The control operator is present at the control point and is continuously monitoring and supervising the third party's participation; and

(2) The third party is not a prior amateur service licensee whose license was revoked or not renewed after hearing and re-licensing has not taken place; suspended for less than the balance of the license term and the suspension is still in effect; suspended for the balance of the license term and re-licensing has not taken place; or surrendered for cancellation following notice of revocation, suspension or monetary forfeiture proceedings. The third party may not be the subject of a cease and desist order

which relates to amateur service operation and which is still in effect.

(c) No station may transmit third party communications while being automatically controlled except a station transmitting a RTTY or data emission.

(d) At the end of an exchange of international third party communications, the station must also transmit in the station identification procedure the call sign of the station with which a third party message was exchanged.

[54 FR 25857, June 20, 1989; 54 FR 39535, Sept. 27, 1989, as amended at 71 FR 25982, May 3, 2006; 71 FR 66462, Nov. 15, 2006]

**§97.117 International communications.**

Transmissions to a different country, where permitted, shall be limited to communications incidental to the purposes of the amateur service and to remarks of a personal character.

[71 FR 25982, May 3, 2006]

## §97.119 Station identification.

(a) Each amateur station, except a space station or telecommand station, must transmit its assigned call sign on its transmitting channel at the end of each communication, and at least every 10 minutes during a communication, for the purpose of clearly making the source of the transmissions from the station known to those receiving the transmissions. No station may transmit unidentified communications or signals, or transmit as the station call sign, any call sign not authorized to the station.

(b) The call sign must be transmitted with an emission authorized for the transmitting channel in one of the following ways:

(1) By a CW emission. When keyed by an automatic device used only for identification, the speed must not exceed 20 words per minute;

(2) By a phone emission in the English language. Use of a phonetic alphabet as an aid for correct station identification is encouraged;

(3) By a RTTY emission using a specified digital code when all or part of the communications are transmitted by a RTTY or data emission;

(4) By an image emission conforming to the applicable transmission standards, either color or monochrome, of §73.682(a) of the FCC Rules when all or part of the communications are transmitted in the same image emission

(c) One or more indicators may be included with the call sign. Each indicator must be separated from the call sign by the slant mark (/) or by any suitable word that denotes the slant mark. If an indicator is self-assigned, it must be included before, after, or both before and after, the call sign. No self-assigned indicator may conflict with any other indicator specified by the FCC Rules or with any prefix assigned to another country.

(d) When transmitting in conjunction with an event of special significance, a station may substitute for its assigned call sign a special event call sign as shown for that station for that period of time on the common data base coordinated, maintained and disseminated by the special event call sign data base coordinators. Additionally, the station must transmit its assigned call sign at least once per hour during such transmissions.

(e) When the operator license class held by the control operator exceeds that of the station licensee, an indicator consisting of the call sign assigned to the control operator's station must be included after the call sign.

(f) When the control operator is a person who is exercising the rights and privileges authorized by §97.9(b) of this part, an indicator must be included after the call sign as follows:

(1) For a control operator who has requested a license modification from Novice Class to Technical Class: KT;

(2) For a control operator who has requested a license modification from Novice or Technician to General Class: AG;

(3) For a control operator who has requested a license modification from Novice, Technician, General, or Advanced Class to Amateur Extra Class: AE.

(g) When the station is transmitting under the authority of §97.107 of this part, an indicator consisting of the appropriate letter-numeral designating the station location must be included before the call sign that was issued to the station by the country granting the license. For an amateur service license granted by the Government of Canada, however, the indicator must be included after the call sign. At least once during each intercommunication, the identification announcement must include the geographical location as nearly as possible by city and state, commonwealth or possession.

[54 FR 25857, June 20, 1989, as amended at 54 FR 39535, Sept. 27, 1989; 55 FR 30457, July 26, 1990; 56 FR 28, Jan. 2, 1991; 62 FR 17567, Apr. 10, 1997; 63 FR 68980, Dec. 14, 1998; 64 FR 51471, Sept. 23, 1999; 66 FR 20752, Apr. 25, 2001; 75 FR 78171, Dec. 15, 2010]

**§97.121 Restricted operation.**

(a) If the operation of an amateur station causes general interference to the reception of transmissions from stations operating in the domestic broadcast service when receivers of good engineering design, including adequate selectivity characteristics, are used to receive such transmissions, and this fact is made known to the amateur station licensee, the amateur station shall not be operated during the hours from 8 p.m. to 10:30 p.m., local time, and on Sunday for the additional period from 10:30 a.m. until 1 p.m., local time, upon the frequency or frequencies used when the interference is created.

(b) In general, such steps as may be necessary to minimize interference to stations operating in other services may be required after investigation by the FCC.

# Subpart C—Special Operations

## §97.201 Auxiliary station.

(a) Any amateur station licensed to a holder of a Technician, General, Advanced or Amateur Extra Class operator license may be an auxiliary station. A holder of a Technician, General, Advanced or Amateur Extra Class operator license may be the control operator of an auxiliary station, subject to the privileges of the class of operator license held.

(b) An auxiliary station may transmit only on the 2 m and shorter wavelength bands, except the 144.0-144.5 MHz, 145.8-146.0 MHz, 219-220 MHz, 222.00-222.15 MHz, 431-433 MHz, and 435-438 MHz segments.

(c) Where an auxiliary station causes harmful interference to another auxiliary station, the licensees are equally and fully responsible for resolving the interference unless one station's operation is recommended by a frequency coordinator and the other station's is not. In that case, the licensee of the non-coordinated auxiliary station has primary responsibility to resolve the interference.

(d) An auxiliary station may be automatically controlled.

(e) An auxiliary station may transmit one-way communications.

[54 FR 25857, June 20, 1989, as amended at 56 FR 56171, Nov. 1, 1991; 60 FR 15687, Mar. 27, 1995; 63 FR 68980, Dec. 14, 1998; 71 FR 66462, Nov. 15, 2006; 75 FR 78171, Dec. 15, 2010]

**§97.203 Beacon station.**

(a) Any amateur station licensed to a holder of a Technician, General, Advanced or Amateur Extra Class operator license may be a beacon. A holder of a Technician, General, Advanced or Amateur Extra Class operator license may be the control operator of a beacon, subject to the privileges of the class of operator license held.

(b) A beacon must not concurrently transmit on more than 1 channel in the same amateur service frequency band, from the same station location.

(c) The transmitter power of a beacon must not exceed 100 W.

(d) A beacon may be automatically controlled while it is transmitting on the 28.20-28.30 MHz, 50.06-50.08 MHz, 144.275-144.300 MHz, 222.05-222.06 MHz or 432.300-432.400 MHz segments, or on the 33 cm and shorter wavelength bands.

(e) Before establishing an automatically controlled beacon in the National Radio Quiet Zone or before changing the transmitting frequency, transmitter power, antenna height or directivity, the station licensee must give written notification thereof to the Interference Office, National Radio Astronomy Observatory, P.O. Box 2, Green Bank, WV 24944.

(1) The notification must include the geographical coordinates of the antenna, antenna ground elevation above mean sea level (AMSL), antenna center of radiation above ground level (AGL), antenna directivity, proposed frequency, type of emission, and transmitter power.

(2) If an objection to the proposed operation is received by the FCC from the National Radio Astronomy Observatory at Green Bank, Pocahontas County, WV, for itself or on behalf of the Naval Research Laboratory at Sugar Grove, Pendleton County, WV, within 20 days from the date of notification, the FCC will consider all aspects of the problem and take whatever action is deemed appropriate.

(f) A beacon must cease transmissions upon notification by a District Director that the station is operating improperly or causing undue interference to other operations. The beacon may not resume transmitting without prior approval of the District Director.

(g) A beacon may transmit one-way communications.

[54 FR 25857, June 20, 1989, as amended at 55 FR 9323, Mar. 13, 1990; 56 FR 19610, Apr. 29, 1991; 56 FR 32517, July 17, 1991; 62 FR 55536, Oct. 27, 1997; 63 FR 41204, Aug. 3, 1998; 63 FR 68980, Dec. 14, 1998; 69 FR 24997, May 5, 2004; 71 FR 66462, Nov. 15, 2006; 75 FR 78171, Dec. 15, 2010]

## §97.205 Repeater station.

(a) Any amateur station licensed to a holder of a Technician, General, Advanced or Amateur Extra Class operator license may be a repeater. A holder of a Technician, General, Advanced or Amateur Extra Class operator license may be the control operator of a repeater, subject to the privileges of the class of operator license held.

(b) A repeater may receive and retransmit only on the 10 m and shorter wavelength frequency bands except the 28.0-29.5 MHz, 50.0-51.0 MHz, 144.0-144.5 MHz, 145.5-146.0 MHz, 222.00-222.15 MHz, 431.0-433.0 Mhz, and 435.0-438.0 Mhz segments.

(c) Where the transmissions of a repeater cause harmful interference to another repeater, the two station licensees are equally and fully responsible for resolving the interference unless the operation of one station is recommended by a frequency coordinator and the operation of the other station is not. In that case, the licensee of the non-coordinated repeater has primary responsibility to resolve the interference.

(d) A repeater may be automatically controlled.

(e) Ancillary functions of a repeater that are available to users on the input channel are not considered remotely controlled functions of the station. Limiting the use of a repeater to only certain user stations is permissible.

(f) [Reserved]

(g) The control operator of a repeater that retransmits inadvertently communications that violate the rules in this part is not accountable for the violative communications.

(h) The provisions of this paragraph do not apply to repeaters that transmit on the 1.2 cm or shorter wavelength bands. Before establishing a repeater within 16 km (10 miles) of the Arecibo Observatory or before changing the transmitting frequency, transmitter power, antenna height or directivity of an existing repeater, the station licensee must give written notification thereof to the Interference Office, Arecibo Observatory, HC3 Box 53995, Arecibo, Puerto Rico 00612, in writing or electronically, of the technical parameters of the proposal. Licensees who choose to transmit information electronically should e-mail to: *prcz@naic.edu.*

(1) The notification shall state the geographical coordinates of the antenna (NAD-83 datum), antenna height above mean sea level (AMSL), antenna center of radiation above ground level (AGL), antenna directivity and gain, proposed frequency and FCC Rule Part, type of emission, effective radiated power, and whether the proposed use is itinerant. Licensees may wish to consult interference guidelines provided by Cornell University.

(2) If an objection to the proposed operation is received by the FCC from the Arecibo Observatory, Arecibo, Puerto Rico, within 20 days from the date of notification, the FCC will consider all aspects of the problem and take whatever action is deemed appropriate. The licensee will be required to make reasonable efforts in order to resolve or mitigate any potential interference problem with the Arecibo Observatory.

[54 FR 25857, June 20, 1989, as amended at 55 FR 4613, Feb. 9, 1990; 56 FR 32517, July 17, 1991; 58 FR 64385, Dec. 7, 1993; 59 FR 18975, Apr. 21, 1994; 62 FR 55536, Oct. 27, 1997; 63 FR 41205, Aug. 3, 1998; 63 FR 68980, Dec. 14, 1998; 69 FR 24997, May 5, 2004; 70 FR 31374, June 1, 2005]

**§97.207 Space station.**

(a) Any amateur station may be a space station. A holder of any class operator license may be the control operator of a space station, subject to the privileges of the class of operator license held by the control operator.

(b) A space station must be capable of effecting a cessation of transmissions by telecommand whenever such cessation is ordered by the FCC.

(c) The following frequency bands and segments are authorized to space stations:

(1) The 17 m, 15 m, 12 m, and 10 m bands, 6 mm, 4 mm, 2 mm and 1 mm bands; and

(2) The 7.0-7.1 MHz, 14.00-14.25 MHz, 144-146 MHz, 435-438 MHz, 2400-2450 MHz, 3.40-3.41 GHz, 5.83-5.85 GHz, 10.45-10.50 GHz, and 24.00-24.05 GHz segments.

(d) A space station may automatically retransmit the radio signals of Earth stations and other space stations.

(e) A space station may transmit one-way communications.

(f) Space telemetry transmissions may consist of specially coded messages intended to facilitate communications or related to the function of the spacecraft.

(g) The license grantee of each space station must make the following written notifications to the International Bureau, FCC, Washington, DC 20554.

(1) A pre-space notification within 30 days after the date of launch vehicle determination, but no later than 90 days before integration of the space station into the launch vehicle. The notification must be in accordance with the provisions of Articles 9 and 11 of the International Telecommunication Union (ITU) Radio Regulations and must specify the information required by Appendix 4 and Resolution No. 642 of the ITU Radio Regulations. The notification must also include a description of the design and operational strategies that the space station will use to mitigate orbital debris, including the following information:

(i) A statement that the space station licensee has assessed and limited the amount of debris released in a planned manner during normal operations, and has assessed and limited the probability of the space station becoming a source of debris by collisions with small debris or meteoroids that could cause loss of control and prevent post-mission disposal;

(ii) A statement that the space station licensee has assessed and limited the probability of accidental explosions during and after completion of mission operations. This statement must include a demonstration that debris generation will not result from the conversion of energy sources on board the spacecraft into energy that fragments the spacecraft. Energy sources include chemical, pressure, and kinetic energy. This demonstration should address whether stored energy will be removed at the spacecraft's end of life, by depleting residual fuel and leaving all fuel line valves open, venting any pressurized system, leaving all batteries in a permanent discharge state, and removing any remaining source of stored energy, or through other equivalent procedures specifically disclosed in the application;

(iii) A statement that the space station licensee has assessed and limited the probability of the space station becoming a source of debris by collisions with large debris or other operational space stations. Where a space station will be launched into a low-Earth orbit that is identical, or very similar, to an orbit used by other space stations, the statement must include an analysis of the potential risk of collision and a description of what measures the space station operator plans to take to avoid in-orbit collisions. If the space station licensee is relying on coordination with another system, the statement must indicate what steps have been taken to contact, and ascertain the likelihood of successful coordination of physical operations with, the other system. The statement must disclose the accuracy—if any—with which orbital parameters of non-geostationary satellite orbit space stations will be maintained, including apogee, perigee, inclination, and the right ascension of the ascending node(s). In the event that a system is not able to maintain orbital tolerances, *i.e.*, it lacks a propulsion system for orbital maintenance, that fact should be included in the debris mitigation disclosure. Such systems must also indicate the anticipated evolution over time of the orbit of the proposed satellite or satellites. Where a space station requests the assignment of a geostationary-Earth orbit location, it must assess whether there are any known satellites located at, or reasonably expected to be located at, the requested orbital location, or assigned in the vicinity of that location, such that the station keeping volumes of the respective satellites might overlap. If so, the statement must include a statement as to the identities of those parties and the measures that will be taken to prevent collisions;

(iv) A statement detailing the post-mission disposal plans for the space station at end of life, including the quantity of fuel—if any—that will be reserved for post-mission disposal maneuvers. For geostationary-Earth orbit space stations, the statement must disclose the altitude selected for a post-mission disposal orbit and the calculations that are used in deriving the disposal altitude.

The statement must also include a casualty risk assessment if planned post-mission disposal involves atmospheric re-entry of the space station. In general, an assessment should include an estimate as to whether portions of the spacecraft will survive re-entry and reach the surface of the Earth, as well as an estimate of the resulting probability of human casualty.

(v) If any material item described in this notification changes before launch, a replacement pre-space notification shall be filed with the International Bureau no later than 90 days before integration of the space station into the launch vehicle.

(2) An in-space station notification is required no later than 7 days following initiation of space station transmissions. This notification must update the information contained in the pre-space notification.

(3) A post-space station notification is required no later than 3 months after termination of the space station transmissions. When termination of transmissions is ordered by the FCC, the notification is required no later than 24 hours after termination of transmissions.

[54 FR 25857, June 20, 1989, as amended at 54 FR 39535, Sept. 27, 1989; 56 FR 56171, Nov. 1, 1991; 57 FR 32736, July 23, 1992; 60 FR 50124, Sept. 28, 1995; 63 FR 68980, Dec. 14, 1998; 69 FR 54588, Sept. 9, 2004; 71 FR 66462, Nov. 15, 2006; 75 FR 27201, May 14, 2010]

**§97.209 Earth station.**

(a) Any amateur station may be an Earth station. A holder of any class operator license may be the control operator of an Earth station, subject to the privileges of the class of operator license held by the control operator.

(b) The following frequency bands and segments are authorized to Earth stations:

(1) The 17 m, 15 m, 12 m, and 10 m bands, 6 mm, 4 mm, 2 mm and 1 mm bands; and

(2) The 7.0-7.1 MHz, 14.00-14.25 MHz, 144-146 MHz, 435-438 MHz, 1260-1270 MHz and 2400-2450 MHz, 3.40-3.41 GHz, 5.65-5.67 GHz, 10.45-10.50 GHz and 24.00-24.05 GHz segments.

[54 FR 25857, June 20, 1989, as amended at 54 FR 39535, Sept. 27, 1989]

## §97.211 Space telecommand station.

(a) Any amateur station designated by the licensee of a space station is eligible to transmit as a telecommand station for that space station, subject to the privileges of the class of operator license held by the control operator.

(b) A telecommand station may transmit special codes intended to obscure the meaning of telecommand messages to the station in space operation.

(c) The following frequency bands and segments are authorized to telecommand stations:

(1) The 17 m, 15 m, 12 m and 10 m bands, 6 mm, 4 mm, 2 mm and 1 mm bands; and

(2) The 7.0-7.1 MHz, 14.00-14.25 MHz, 144-146 MHz, 435-438 MHz, 1260-1270 MHz and 2400-2450 MHz, 3.40-3.41 GHz, 5.65-5.67 GHz, 10.45-10.50 GHz and 24.00-24.05 GHz segments.

(d) A telecommand station may transmit one-way communications.

[54 FR 25857, June 20, 1989, as amended at 54 FR 39535, Sept. 27, 1989; 56 FR 56171, Nov. 1, 1991]

## §97.213 Telecommand of an amateur station.

An amateur station on or within 50 km of the Earth's surface may be under telecommand where:

(a) There is a radio or wireline control link between the control point and the station sufficient for the control operator to perform his/her duties. If radio, the control link must use an auxiliary station. A control link using a fiber optic cable or another telecommunication service is considered wireline.

(b) Provisions are incorporated to limit transmission by the station to a period of no more than 3 minutes in the event of malfunction in the control link.

(c) The station is protected against making, willfully or negligently, unauthorized transmissions.

(d) A photocopy of the station license and a label with the name, address, and telephone number of the station licensee and at least one designated control operator is posted in a conspicuous place at the station location.

[54 FR 25857, June 20, 1989, as amended at 56 FR 56171, Nov. 1, 1991]

### §97.215 Telecommand of model craft.

An amateur station transmitting signals to control a model craft may be operated as follows:

(a) The station identification procedure is not required for transmissions directed only to the model craft, provided that a label indicating the station call sign and the station licensee's name and address is affixed to the station transmitter.

(b) The control signals are not considered codes or ciphers intended to obscure the meaning of the communication.

(c) The transmitter power must not exceed 1 W.

[54 FR 25857, June 20, 1989, as amended at 56 FR 56171, Nov. 1, 1991]

*Amateur Radio Service, Part 97*

**§97.217 Telemetry.**

Telemetry transmitted by an amateur station on or within 50 km of the Earth's surface is not considered to be codes or ciphers intended to obscure the meaning of communications.

[56 FR 56172, Nov. 1, 1991. Redesignated at 59 FR 18975, Apr. 21, 1994]

## §97.219 Message forwarding system.

(a) Any amateur station may participate in a message forwarding system, subject to the privileges of the class of operator license held.

(b) For stations participating in a message forwarding system, the control operator of the station originating a message is primarily accountable for any violation of the rules in this part contained in the message.

(c) Except as noted in (d) of this section, for stations participating in a message forwarding system, the control operators of forwarding stations that retransmit inadvertently communications that violate the rules in this part are not accountable for the violative communications. They are, however, responsible for discontinuing such communications once they become aware of their presence.

(d) For stations participating in a message forwarding system, the control operator of the first forwarding station must:

(1) Authenticate the identity of the station from which it accepts communications on behalf of the system; or

(2) Accept accountability for any violation of the rules in this part contained in messages it retransmits to the system.

[59 FR 18975, Apr. 21, 1994]

### §97.221 Automatically controlled digital station.

(a) This rule section does not apply to an auxiliary station, a beacon station, a repeater station, an earth station, a space station, or a space telecommand station.

(b) A station may be automatically controlled while transmitting a RTTY or data emission on the 6 m or shorter wavelength bands, and on the 28.120-28.189 MHz, 24.925-24.930 MHz, 21.090-21.100 MHz, 18.105-18.110 MHz, 14.0950-14.0995 MHz, 14.1005-14.112 MHz, 10.140-10.150 MHz, 7.100-7.105 MHz, or 3.585-3.600 MHz segments.

(c) Except for channels specified in §97.303(h), a station may be automatically controlled while transmitting a RTTY or data emission on any other frequency authorized for such emission types provided that:

(1) The station is responding to interrogation by a station under local or remote control; and

(2) No transmission from the automatically controlled station occupies a bandwidth of more than 500 Hz.

[60 FR 26001, May 16, 1995, as amended at 72 FR 3082, Jan. 24, 2007; 77 FR 5412, Feb. 3, 2012]

# Subpart D—Technical Standards

### §97.301 Authorized frequency bands.

The following transmitting frequency bands are available to an amateur station located within 50 km of the Earth's surface, within the specified ITU Region, and outside any area where the amateur service is regulated by any authority other than the FCC.

(a) For a station having a control operator who has been granted a Technician, General, Advanced, or Amateur Extra Class operator license or who holds a CEPT radio-amateur license or IARP of any class:

| Wavelength band | ITU region 1 | ITU region 2 | ITU region 3 | Sharing requirements *see* §97.303 (paragraph) |
|---|---|---|---|---|
| **VHF** | **MHz** | **MHz** | **MHz** | |
| 6 m | | 50-54 | 50-54 | (a) |
| 2 m | 144-146 | 144-148 | 144-148 | (a), (k) |
| 1.25 m | | 219-220 | | (l) |
| Do | | 222-225 | | (a) |
| **UHF** | **MHz** | **MHz** | **MHz** | |
| 70 cm | 430-440 | 420-450 | 430-440 | (a), (b), (m) |
| 33 cm | | 902-928 | | (a), (b), (e), (n) |
| 23 cm | 1240-1300 | 1240-1300 | 1240-1300 | (b), (d), (o) |
| 13 cm | 2300-2310 | 2300-2310 | 2300-2310 | (d), (p) |
| Do | 2390-2450 | 2390-2450 | 2390-2450 | (d), (e), (p) |
| **SHF** | **GHz** | **GHz** | **GHz** | |
| 9 cm | | 3.3-3.5 | 3.3-3.5 | (a), (b), (f), (q) |
| 5 cm | 5.650-5.850 | 5.650-5.925 | 5.650-5.850 | (a), (b), (e), (r) |
| 3 cm | 10.0-10.5 | 10.0-10.5 | 10.0-10.5 | (a), (b), (k) |
| 1.2 cm | 24.00-24.25 | 24.00-24.25 | 24.00-24.25 | (b), (d), (e) |
| **EHF** | **GHz** | **GHz** | **GHz** | |
| 6 mm | 47.0-47.2 | 47.0-47.2 | 47.0-47.2 | |

| 4 mm | 76-81 | 76-81 | 76-81 | (c), (f), (s) |
|---|---|---|---|---|
| 2.5 mm | 122.25-123.00 | 122.25-123.00 | 122.25-123.00 | (e), (t) |
| 2 mm | 134-141 | 134-141 | 134-141 | (c), (f) |
| 1 mm | 241-250 | 241-250 | 241-250 | (c), (e), (f) |
|  | Above 275 | Above 275 | Above 275 | (f) |

(b) For a station having a control operator who has been granted an Amateur Extra Class operator license, who holds a CEPT radio amateur license, or who holds a Class 1 IARP license:

| Wavelength band | ITU region 1 | ITU region 2 | ITU region 3 | Sharing requirements *see* §97.303 |
|---|---|---|---|---|
| MF | kHz | kHz | kHz | (paragraph) |
| 160 m | 1810-1850 | 1800-2000 | 1800-2000 | (a), (c), (g) |
| HF | MHz | MHz | MHz | |
| 80 m | 3.500-3.600 | 3.500-3.600 | 3.500-3.600 | (a) |
| 75 m | 3.600-3.800 | 3.600-4.000 | 3.600-3.900 | (a) |
| 60 m | | See §97.303(h) | | (h) |
| 40 m | 7.000-7.200 | 7.000-7.300 | 7.000-7.200 | (i) |
| 30 m | 10.100-10.150 | 10.100-10.150 | 10.100-10.150 | (j) |
| 20 m | 14.000-14.350 | 14.000-14.350 | 14.000-14.350 | |
| 17 m | 18.068-18.168 | 18.068-18.168 | 18.068-18.168 | |
| 15 m | 21.000-21.450 | 21.000-21.450 | 21.000-21.450 | |
| 12 m | 24.890-24.990 | 24.890-24.990 | 24.890-24.990 | |
| 10 m | 28.000-29.700 | 28.000-29.700 | 28.000-29.700 | |

(c) For a station having a control operator who has been granted an operator license of Advanced Class:

| Wavelength band | ITU region 1 | ITU region 2 | ITU region 3 | Sharing requirements *see* §97.303 (Paragraph) |
|---|---|---|---|---|
| **MF** | kHz | kHz | kHz | |
| 160 m | 1810-1850 | 1800-2000 | 1800-2000 | (a), (c), (g) |
| **HF** | **MHz** | **MHz** | **MHz** | |
| 80 m | 3.525-3.600 | 3.525-3.600 | 3.525-3.600 | (a) |
| 75 m | 3.700-3.800 | 3.700-4.000 | 3.700-3.900 | (a) |
| 60 m | | See §97.303(h) | | (h) |
| 40 m | 7.025-7.200 | 7.025-7.300 | 7.025-7.200 | (i) |
| 30 m | 10.100-10.150 | 10.100-10.150 | 10.100-10.150 | (j) |
| 20 m | 14.025-14.150 | 14.025-14.150 | 14.025-14.150 | |
| Do | 14.175-14.350 | 14.175-14.350 | 14.175-14.350 | |
| 17 m | 18.068-18.168 | 18.068-18.168 | 18.068-18.168 | |
| 15 m | 21.025-21.200 | 21.025-21.200 | 21.025-21.200 | |
| Do | 21.225-21.450 | 21.225-21.450 | 21.225-21.450 | |
| 12 m | 24.890-24.990 | 24.890-24.990 | 24.890-24.990 | |

## Amateur Radio Service, Part 97

| 10 m | 28.000-29.700 | 28.000-29.700 | 28.000-29.700 | |
|------|---------------|---------------|---------------|--|

(d) For a station having a control operator who has been granted an operator license of General Class:

| Wavelength band | ITU region 1 | ITU region 2 | ITU region 3 | Sharing requirements *see* §97.303 (paragraph) |
|---|---|---|---|---|
| MF | kHz | kHz | kHz | |
| 160 m | 1810-1850 | 1800-2000 | 1800-2000 | (a), (c), (g) |
| HF | MHz | MHz | MHz | |
| 80 m | 3.525-3.600 | 3.525-3.600 | 3.525-3.600 | (a) |
| 75 m | | 3.800-4.000 | 3.800-3.900 | (a) |
| 60 m | | See §97.303(h) | | (h) |
| 40 m | 7.025-7.125 | 7.025-7.125 | 7.025-7.125 | (i) |
| Do | 7.175-7.200 | 7.175-7.300 | 7.175-7.200 | (i) |
| 30 m | 10.100-10.150 | 10.100-10.150 | 10.100-10.150 | (j) |
| 20 m | 14.025-14.150 | 14.025-14.150 | 14.025-14.150 | |
| Do | 14.225-14.350 | 14.225-14.350 | 14.225-14.350 | |
| 17 m | 18.068-18.168 | 18.068-18.168 | 18.068-18.168 | |
| 15 m | 21.025-21.200 | 21.025-21.200 | 21.025-21.200 | |
| Do | 21.275-21.450 | 21.275-21.450 | 21.275-21.450 | |

| 12 m | 24.890-24.990 | 24.890-24.990 | 24.890-24.990 | |
|------|---------------|---------------|---------------|--|
| 10 m | 28.000-29.700 | 28.000-29.700 | 28.000-29.700 | |

(e) For a station having a control operator who has been granted an operator license of Novice Class or Technician Class:

| Wavelength band | ITU region 1 | ITU region 2 | ITU region 3 | Sharing requirements *see* §97.303 (paragraph) |
|---|---|---|---|---|
| **HF** | **MHz** | **MHz** | **MHz** | |
| 80 m | 3.525-3.600 | 3.525-3.600 | 3.525-3.600 | (a) |
| 40 m | 7.025-7.125 | 7.025-7.125 | 7.025-7.125 | (i) |
| 15 m | 21.025-21.200 | 21.025-21.200 | 21.025-21.200 | |
| 10 m | 28.0-28.5 | 28.0-28.5 | 28.0-28.5 | |
| **VHF** | **MHz** | **MHz** | **MHz** | |
| 1.25 m | | 222-225 | | (a) |
| **UHF** | **MHz** | **MHz** | **MHz** | |
| 23 cm | 1270-1295 | 1270-1295 | 1270-1295 | (d), (o) |

[75 FR 27201, May 14, 2010, as amended at 75 FR 78171, Dec. 15, 2010]

## §97.303 Frequency sharing requirements.

The following paragraphs summarize the frequency sharing requirements that apply to amateur stations transmitting in the frequency bands specified in §97.301 of this part. Each frequency band allocated to the amateur service is designated as either a secondary service or a primary service. A station in a secondary service must not cause harmful interference to, and must accept interference from, stations in a primary service.

(a) Where, in adjacent ITU Regions or sub-Regions, a band of frequencies is allocated to different services of the same category (*i.e.,* primary or secondary services), the basic principle is the equality of right to operate. Accordingly, stations of each service in one Region or sub-Region must operate so as not to cause harmful interference to any service of the same or higher category in the other Regions or sub-Regions.

(b) Amateur stations transmitting in the 70 cm band, the 33 cm band, the 23 cm band, the 9 cm band, the 5 cm band, the 3 cm band, or the 24.05-24.25 GHz segment must not cause harmful interference to, and must accept interference from, stations authorized by the United States Government in the radiolocation service.

(c) Amateur stations transmitting in the 1900-2000 kHz segment, the 76-77.5 GHz segment, the 78-81 GHz segment, the 136-141 GHz segment, or the 241-248 GHz segment must not cause harmful interference to, and must accept interference from, stations authorized by the United States Government, the FCC, or other nations in the radiolocation service.

(d) Amateur stations transmitting in the 430-450 MHz segment, the 23 cm band, the 3.3-3.4 GHz segment, the

5.65-5.85 GHz segment, the 13 cm band, or the 24.05-24.25 GHz segment, must not cause harmful interference to, and must accept interference from, stations authorized by other nations in the radiolocation service.

(e) Amateur stations receiving in the 33 cm band, the 2400-2450 MHz segment, the 5.725-5.875 GHz segment, the 1.2 cm band, the 2.5 mm band, or the 244-246 GHz segment must accept interference from industrial, scientific, and medical (ISM) equipment.

(f) Amateur stations transmitting in the following segments must not cause harmful interference to radio astronomy stations: 3.332-3.339 GHz, 3.3458-3.3525 GHz, 76-77.5 GHz, 78-81 GHz, 136-141 GHz, 241-248 GHz, 275-323 GHz, 327-371 GHz, 388-424 GHz, 426-442 GHz, 453-510 GHz, 623-711 GHz, 795-909 GHz, or 926-945 GHz. In addition, amateur stations transmitting in the following segments must not cause harmful interference to stations in the Earth exploration-satellite service (passive) or the space research service (passive): 275-277 GHz, 294-306 GHz, 316-334 GHz, 342-349 GHz, 363-365 GHz, 371-389 GHz, 416-434 GHz, 442-444 GHz, 496-506 GHz, 546-568 GHz, 624-629 GHz, 634-654 GHz, 659-661 GHz, 684-692 GHz, 730-732 GHz, 851-853 GHz, or 951-956 GHz.

(g) Amateur stations transmitting in the 1900-2000 kHz segment must not cause harmful interference to, and must accept interference from, stations authorized by other nations in the fixed, mobile except aeronautical mobile, and radio navigation services.

(h) *60 m band:* (1) In the 5330.5-5406.4 kHz band (60 m band), amateur stations may transmit only on the five center frequencies specified in the table below. In order to meet this requirement, control operators of stations transmitting phone, data, and RTTY emissions (emission designators 2K80J3E, 2K80J2D, and 60H0J2B, respectively) may set the carrier frequency 1.5 kHz below the center frequency as specified in the table below. For CW emissions (emission designator 150HA1A), the carrier frequency is set to the center frequency. Amateur operators shall ensure that their emissions do not occupy more than 2.8 kHz centered on each of these center frequencies.

### 60 M BAND FREQUENCIES (KHZ)

| Carrier | Center |
|---------|--------|
| 5330.5 | 5332.0 |
| 5346.5 | 5348.0 |
| 5357.0 | 5358.5 |
| 5371.5 | 5373.0 |
| 5403.5 | 5405.0 |

(2) Amateur stations transmitting on the 60 m band must not cause harmful interference to, and must accept interference from, stations authorized by:

(i) The United States (NTIA and FCC) and other nations in the fixed service; and

(ii) Other nations in the mobile except aeronautical mobile service.

(i) Amateur stations transmitting in the 7.2-7.3 MHz segment must not cause harmful interference to, and must accept interference from, international broadcast stations whose programming is intended for use within Region 1 or Region 3.

(j) Amateur stations transmitting in the 30 m band must not cause harmful interference to, and must accept interference from, stations by other nations in the fixed service. The licensee of the amateur station must make all necessary adjustments, including termination of transmissions, if harmful interference is caused.

(k) For amateur stations located in ITU Regions 1 and 3: Amateur stations transmitting in the 146-148 MHz segment or the 10.00-10.45 GHz segment must not cause harmful interference to, and must accept interference from, stations of other nations in the fixed and mobile services.

(l) *In the 219-220 MHz segment:*

(1) Use is restricted to amateur stations participating as forwarding stations in fixed point-to-point digital message forwarding systems, including intercity packet backbone networks. It is not available for other purposes.

(2) Amateur stations must not cause harmful interference to, and must accept interference from, stations authorized by:

(i) The FCC in the Automated Maritime Telecommunications System (AMTS), the 218-219 MHz Service, and the 220 MHz Service, and television stations broadcasting on channels 11 and 13; and

(ii) Other nations in the fixed and maritime mobile services.

(3) No amateur station may transmit unless the licensee has given written notification of the station's specific geographic location for such transmissions in order to be incorporated into a database that has been made available to the public. The notification must be given at

least 30 days prior to making such transmissions. The notification must be given to: The American Radio Relay League, Inc., 225 Main Street, Newington, CT 06111-1494.

(4) No amateur station may transmit from a location that is within 640 km of an AMTS coast station that operates in the 217-218 MHz and 219-220 MHz bands unless the amateur station licensee has given written notification of the station's specific geographic location for such transmissions to the AMTS licensee. The notification must be given at least 30 days prior to making such transmissions. The location of AMTS coast stations using the 217-218/219-220 MHz channels may be obtained as noted in paragraph (l)(3) of this section.

(5) No amateur station may transmit from a location that is within 80 km of an AMTS coast station that uses frequencies in the 217-218 MHz and 219-220 MHz bands unless that amateur station licensee holds written approval from that AMTS licensee. The location of AMTS coast stations using the 217-218/219-220 MHz channels may be obtained as noted in paragraph (l)(3) of this section.

(m) *In the 70 cm band:*

(1) No amateur station shall transmit from north of Line A in the 420-430 MHz segment. See §97.3(a) for the definition of Line A.

(2) Amateur stations transmitting in the 420-430 MHz segment must not cause harmful interference to, and must accept interference from, stations authorized by the FCC in the land mobile service within 80.5 km of Buffalo, Cleveland, and Detroit. See §2.106, footnote US230 for specific frequencies and coordinates.

(3) Amateur stations transmitting in the 420-430 MHz segment or the 440-450 MHz segment must not cause harmful interference to, and must accept interference from, stations authorized by other nations in the fixed and mobile except aeronautical mobile services.

(n) *In the 33 cm band:*

(1) Amateur stations must not cause harmful interference to, and must accept interference from, stations authorized by:

(i) The United States Government;

(ii) The FCC in the Location and Monitoring Service; and

(iii) Other nations in the fixed service.

(2) No amateur station shall transmit from those portions of Texas and New Mexico that are bounded by latitudes 31°41′ and 34°30′ North and longitudes 104°11′ and 107°30′ West; or from outside of the United States and its Region 2 insular areas.

(3) No amateur station shall transmit from those portions of Colorado and Wyoming that are bounded by latitudes 39° and 42° North and longitudes 103° and 108° West in the following segments: 902.4-902.6 MHz, 904.3-904.7 MHz, 925.3-925.7 MHz, and 927.3-927.7 MHz.

(o) Amateur stations transmitting in the 23 cm band must not cause harmful interference to, and must accept interference from, stations authorized by:

*Amateur Radio Service, Part 97*

(1) The United States Government in the aeronautical radio navigation, Earth exploration-satellite (active), or space research (active) services;

(2) The FCC in the aeronautical radio navigation service; and

(3) Other nations in the Earth exploration-satellite (active), radio navigation-satellite (space-to-Earth) (space-to-space), or space research (active) services.

(p) *In the 13 cm band:*

(1) Amateur stations must not cause harmful interference to, and must accept interference from, stations authorized by other nations in fixed and mobile services.

(2) Amateur stations transmitting in the 2305-2310 MHz segment must not cause harmful interference to, and must accept interference from, stations authorized by the FCC in the fixed, mobile except aeronautical mobile, and radiolocation services.

(q) Amateur stations transmitting in the 3.4-3.5 GHz segment must not cause harmful interference to, and must accept interference from, stations authorized by other nations in the fixed and fixed-satellite (space-to-Earth) services.

(r) *In the 5 cm band:*

(1) Amateur stations transmitting in the 5.650-5.725 GHz segment must not cause harmful interference to, and must accept interference from, stations authorized by other nations in the mobile except aeronautical mobile service.

(2) Amateur stations transmitting in the 5.850-5.925 GHz segment must not cause harmful interference to, and must accept interference from, stations authorized by the FCC and other nations in the fixed-satellite (Earth-to-space) and mobile services and also stations authorized by other nations in the fixed service. In the United States, the use of mobile service is restricted to Dedicated Short Range Communications operating in the Intelligent Transportation System.

(s) Authorization of the 76-77 GHz segment for amateur station transmissions is suspended until such time that the Commission may determine that amateur station transmissions in this segment will not pose a safety threat to vehicle radar systems operating in this segment.

(t) Amateur stations transmitting in the 2.5 mm band must not cause harmful interference to, and must accept interference from, stations authorized by the United States Government, the FCC, or other nations in the fixed, inter-satellite, or mobile services.

NOTE TO §97.303: The Table of Frequency Allocations contains the complete, unabridged, and legally binding frequency sharing requirements that pertain to the Amateur Radio Service. *See* 47 CFR 2.104, 2.105, and 2.106. The United States, Puerto Rico, and the U.S. Virgin Islands are in Region 2 and other U.S. insular areas are in either Region 2 or 3; see appendix 1 to part 97.

[75 FR 27203, May 14, 2010, as amended at 77 FR 5412, Feb. 3, 2012]

## §97.305 Authorized emission types.

(a) Except as specified elsewhere in this part, an amateur station may transmit a CW emission on any frequency authorized to the control operator.

(b) A station may transmit a test emission on any frequency authorized to the control operator for brief periods for experimental purposes, except that no pulse modulation emission may be transmitted on any frequency where pulse is not specifically authorized and no SS modulation emission may be transmitted on any frequency where SS is not specifically authorized.

(c) A station may transmit the following emission types on the frequencies indicated, as authorized to the control operator, subject to the standards specified in §97.307(f) of this part.

| Wavelength band | Frequencies | Emission types authorized | Standards see §97.307(f), paragraph: |
|---|---|---|---|
| MF: | | | |
| 160 m | Entire band | RTTY, data | (3). |
| 160 m | Entire band | Phone, image | (1), (2). |
| HF: | | | |
| 80 m | Entire band | RTTY, data | (3), (9). |
| 75 m | Entire band | Phone, image | (1), (2). |
| 60 m | 5.332, 5.348, 5.3585, 5.373 and 5.405 MHz | Phone, RTTY, data | (14). |
| 40 m | 7.000-7.100 MHz | RTTY, data | (3), (9) |
| 40 m | 7.075-7.100 MHz | Phone, image | (1), (2), (9), (11) |
| 40 m | 7.100-7.125 MHz | RTTY, data | (3), (9) |
| 40 m | 7.125-7.300 MHz | Phone, image | (1), (2) |
| 30 m | Entire band | RTTY, data | (3). |
| 20 m | 14.00-14.15 MHz | RTTY, data | (3). |
| 20 m | 14.15-14.35 MHz | Phone, image | (1), (2). |
| 17 m | 18.068-18.110 MHz | RTTY, data | (3). |
| 17 m | 18.110-18.168 | Phone, image | (1), (2). |

|  |  | MHz |  |  |
|---|---|---|---|---|
|  | 15 m | 21.0-21.2 MHz | RTTY, data | (3), (9). |
|  | 15 m | 21.20-21.45 MHz | Phone, image | (1), (2). |
|  | 12 m | 24.89-24.93 MHz | RTTY, data | (3). |
|  | 12 m | 24.93-24.99 MHz | Phone, image | (1), (2). |
|  | 10 m | 28.0-28.3 MHz | RTTY, data | (4). |
|  | 10 m | 28.3-28.5 MHz | Phone, image | (1), (2), (10). |
|  | 10 m | 28.5-29.0 MHz | Phone, image | (1), (2). |
|  | 10 m | 29.0-29.7 MHz | Phone, image | (2). |
| VHF: |  |  |  |  |
|  | 6 m | 50.1-51.0 MHz | MCW, phone, image, RTTY, data | (2), (5). |
|  | Do | 51.0-54.0 MHz | MCW, phone, image, RTTY, data, test | (2), (5), (8). |
|  | 2 m | 144.1-148.0 MHz | MCW, phone, image, RTTY, data, test | (2), (5), (8). |
| 1.25 m |  | 219-220 MHz | Data | (13) |
| Do |  | 222-225 MHz | RTTY, data, test MCW, phone, SS, image | (2), (6), (8) |
| UHF: |  |  |  |  |
|  | 70 cm | Entire band | MCW, phone, image, RTTY, data, SS, test | (6), (8). |

| | | | |
|---|---|---|---|
| 33 cm | Entire band | MCW, phone, image, RTTY, data, SS, test, pulse | (7), (8), and (12). |
| 23 cm | Entire band | MCW, phone, image, RTTY, data, SS, test | (7), (8), and (12). |
| 13 cm | Entire band | MCW, phone, image, RTTY, data, SS, test, pulse | (7), (8), and (12). |
| SHF: | | | |
| 9 cm | Entire band | MCW, phone, image, RTTY, data, SS, test, pulse | (7), (8), and (12). |
| 5 cm | Entire band | MCW, phone, image, RTTY, data, SS, test, pulse | (7), (8), and (12). |
| 3 cm | Entire band | MCW, phone, image, RTTY, data, SS, test | (7), (8), and (12). |
| 1.2 cm | Entire band | MCW, phone, image, RTTY, data, SS, test, pulse | (7), (8), and (12). |
| EHF: | | | |
| 6 mm | Entire band | MCW, phone, image, RTTY, data, SS, test, pulse | (7), (8), and (12). |
| 4 mm | Entire band | MCW, phone, image, RTTY, data, SS, test, | (7), (8), and (12). |

| | | pulse | |
|---|---|---|---|
| 2.5 mm | Entire band | MCW, phone, image, RTTY, data, SS, test, pulse | (7), (8), and (12). |
| 2 mm | Entire band | MCW, phone, image, RTTY, data, SS, test, pulse | (7), (8), and (12). |
| 1mm | Entire band | MCW, phone, image, RTTY, data, SS, test, pulse | (7), (8), and (12). |
| | Above 275 GHz | MCW, phone, image, RTTY, data, SS, test, pulse | (7), (8), and (12). |

[54 FR 25857, June 20, 1989; 54 FR 39536, Sept. 27, 1989; 55 FR 22013, May 30, 1990, as amended at 55 FR 30457, July 26, 1990; 60 FR 15688, Mar. 27, 1995; 64 FR 51471, Sept. 23, 1999; 71 FR 66465, Nov. 15, 2006; 75 FR 27204, May 14, 2010; 77 FR 5412, Feb. 3, 2012]

## §97.307 Emission standards.

(a) No amateur station transmission shall occupy more bandwidth than necessary for the information rate and emission type being transmitted, in accordance with good amateur practice.

(b) Emissions resulting from modulation must be confined to the band or segment available to the control operator. Emissions outside the necessary bandwidth must not cause splatter or keyclick interference to operations on adjacent frequencies.

(c) All spurious emissions from a station transmitter must be reduced to the greatest extent practicable. If any spurious emission, including chassis or power line radiation, causes harmful interference to the reception of another radio station, the licensee of the interfering amateur station is required to take steps to eliminate the interference, in accordance with good engineering practice.

(d) For transmitters installed after January 1, 2003, the mean power of any spurious emission from a station transmitter or external RF power amplifier transmitting on a frequency below 30 MHz must be at least 43 dB below the mean power of the fundamental emission. For transmitters installed on or before January 1, 2003, the mean power of any spurious emission from a station transmitter or external RF power amplifier transmitting on a frequency below 30 MHz must not exceed 50 mW and must be at least 40 dB below the mean power of the fundamental emission. For a transmitter of mean power less than 5 W installed on or before January 1, 2003, the attenuation must be at least 30 dB. A transmitter built before April 15, 1977, or first marketed before January 1, 1978, is exempt from this requirement.

(e) The mean power of any spurious emission from a station transmitter or external RF power amplifier transmitting on a frequency between 30-225 MHz must be at least 60 dB below the mean power of the fundamental. For a transmitter having a mean power of 25 W or less, the mean power of any spurious emission supplied to the antenna transmission line must not exceed 25 µW and must be at least 40 dB below the mean power of the fundamental emission, but need not be reduced below the power of 10 µW. A transmitter built before April 15, 1977, or first marketed before January 1, 1978, is exempt from this requirement.

(f) The following standards and limitations apply to transmissions on the frequencies specified in §97.305(c) of this part.

(1) No angle-modulated emission may have a modulation index greater than 1 at the highest modulation frequency.

(2) No non-phone emission shall exceed the bandwidth of a communications quality phone emission of the same modulation type. The total bandwidth of an independent sideband emission (having B as the first symbol), or a multiplexed image and phone emission, shall not exceed that of a communications quality A3E emission.

(3) Only a RTTY or data emission using a specified digital code listed in §97.309(a) of this part may be transmitted. The symbol rate must not exceed 300 bauds, or for frequency-shift keying, the frequency shift between mark and space must not exceed 1 kHz.

(4) Only a RTTY or data emission using a specified digital code listed in §97.309(a) of this part may be transmitted. The symbol rate must not exceed 1200 bauds,

or for frequency-shift keying, the frequency shift between mark and space must not exceed 1 kHz.

(5) A RTTY, data or multiplexed emission using a specified digital code listed in §97.309(a) of this part may be transmitted. The symbol rate must not exceed 19.6 kilobauds. A RTTY, data or multiplexed emission using an unspecified digital code under the limitations listed in §97.309(b) of this part also may be transmitted. The authorized bandwidth is 20 kHz.

(6) A RTTY, data or multiplexed emission using a specified digital code listed in §97.309(a) of this part may be transmitted. The symbol rate must not exceed 56 kilobauds. A RTTY, data or multiplexed emission using an unspecified digital code under the limitations listed in §97.309(b) of this part also may be transmitted. The authorized bandwidth is 100 kHz.

(7) A RTTY, data or multiplexed emission using a specified digital code listed in §97.309(a) of this part or an unspecified digital code under the limitations listed in §97.309(b) of this part may be transmitted.

(8) A RTTY or data emission having designators with A, B, C, D, E, F, G, H, J or R as the first symbol; 1, 2, 7 or 9 as the second symbol; and D or W as the third symbol is also authorized.

(9) A station having a control operator holding a Novice or Technician Class operator license may only transmit a CW emission using the international Morse code.

(10) A station having a control operator holding a Novice Class operator license or a Technician Class operator license and who has received credit for

proficiency in telegraphy in accordance with the international requirements may only transmit a CW emission using the international Morse code or phone emissions J3E and R3E.

(11) Phone and image emissions may be transmitted only by stations located in ITU Regions 1 and 3, and by stations located within ITU Region 2 that are west of 130° West longitude or south of 20° North latitude.

(12) Emission F8E may be transmitted.

(13) A data emission using an unspecified digital code under the limitations listed in §97.309(b) also may be transmitted. The authorized bandwidth is 100 kHz.

(14) *In the 60 m band:*

(i) A station may transmit only phone, RTTY, data, and CW emissions using the emission designators and any additional restrictions that are specified in the table below (except that the use of a narrower necessary bandwidth is permitted):

## 60 M BAND EMISSION REQUIREMENTS

| Emission type | Emission designator | Restricted to: |
|---|---|---|
| Phone | 2K80J3E | Upper sideband transmissions (USB). |
| Data | 2K80J2D | USB (for example, PACTOR-III). |
| RTTY | 60H0J2B | USB (for example, PSK31). |
| CW | 150HA1A | Morse telegraphy by means of on-off keying. |

(ii) The following requirements also apply:

(A) When transmitting the phone, RTTY, and data emissions, the suppressed carrier frequency may be set as specified in §97.303(h).

(B) The control operator of a station transmitting data or RTTY emissions must exercise care to limit the length of transmission so as to avoid causing harmful interference to United States Government stations.

[54 FR 25857, June 20, 1989; 54 FR 30823, July 24, 1989; as amended at 54 FR 39537, Sept. 27, 1989; 60 FR 15688, Mar. 27, 1995; 65 FR 6550, Feb. 10, 2000; 69 FR 24997, May 5, 2004; 77 FR 5412, Feb. 3, 2012]

**§97.309 RTTY and data emission codes.**

(a) Where authorized by §§97.305(c) and 97.307(f) of the part, an amateur station may transmit a RTTY or data emission using the following specified digital codes:

(1) The 5-unit, start-stop, International Telegraph Alphabet No. 2, code defined in ITU-T Recommendation F.1, Division C (commonly known as "Baudot").

(2) The 7-unit code specified in ITU-R Recommendations M.476-5 and M.625-3 (commonly known as "AMTOR").

(3) The 7-unit, International Alphabet No. 5, code defined in IT--T Recommendation T.50 (commonly known as "ASCII").

(4) An amateur station transmitting a RTTY or data emission using a digital code specified in this paragraph may use any technique whose technical characteristics have been documented publicly, such as CLOVER, G-TOR, or PacTOR, for the purpose of facilitating communications.

(b) Where authorized by §§97.305(c) and 97.307(f) of this part, a station may transmit a RTTY or data emission using an unspecified digital code, except to a station in a country with which the United States does not have an agreement permitting the code to be used. RTTY and data emissions using unspecified digital codes must not be transmitted for the purpose of obscuring the meaning of any communication. When deemed necessary by a District Director to assure compliance with the FCC Rules, a station must:

(1) Cease the transmission using the unspecified digital code;

(2) Restrict transmissions of any digital code to the extent instructed;

(3) Maintain a record, convertible to the original information, of all digital communications transmitted.

[54 FR 25857, June 20, 1989, as amended at 54 FR 39537, Sept. 27, 1989; 56 FR 56172, Nov. 1, 1991; 60 FR 55486, Nov. 1, 1995; 71 FR 25982, May 3, 2006; 71 FR 66465, Nov. 15, 2006]

**§97.311 SS emission types.**

(a) SS emission transmissions by an amateur station are authorized only for communications between points within areas where the amateur service is regulated by the FCC and between an area where the amateur service is regulated by the FCC and an amateur station in another country that permits such communications. SS emission transmissions must not be used for the purpose of obscuring the meaning of any communication.

(b) A station transmitting SS emissions must not cause harmful interference to stations employing other authorized emissions, and must accept all interference caused by stations employing other authorized emissions.

(c) When deemed necessary by a District Director to assure compliance with this part, a station licensee must:

(1) Cease SS emission transmissions;

(2) Restrict SS emission transmissions to the extent instructed; and

(3) Maintain a record, convertible to the original information (voice, text, image, etc.) of all spread spectrum communications transmitted.

[64 FR 51471, Sept. 23, 1999, as amended at 76 FR 17569, Mar. 30, 2011]

## §97.313 Transmitter power standards.

(a) An amateur station must use the minimum transmitter power necessary to carry out the desired communications.

(b) No station may transmit with a transmitter power exceeding 1.5 kW PEP.

(c) No station may transmit with a transmitter power output exceeding 200 W PEP:

(1) On the 10.10-10.15 MHz segment;

(2) On the 3.525-3.60 MHz, 7.025-7.125 MHz, 21.025-21.20 MHz, and 28.0-28.5 MHz segment when the control operator is a Novice Class operator or a Technician Class operator; or

(3) The 7.050-7.075 MHz segment when the station is within ITU Regions 1 or 3.

(d) No station may transmit with a transmitter power exceeding 25 W PEP on the VHF 1.25 m band when the control operator is a Novice operator.

(e) No station may transmit with a transmitter power exceeding 5 W PEP on the UHF 23 cm band when the control operator is a Novice operator.

(f) No station may transmit with a transmitter power exceeding 50 W PEP on the UHF 70 cm band from an area specified in paragraph (a) of footnote US270 in §2.106, unless expressly authorized by the FCC after mutual agreement, on a case-by-case basis, between the District Director of the applicable field facility and the military area frequency coordinator at the applicable military base. An Earth station or telecommand station, however, may transmit on the 435-438 MHz segment with a maximum of 611 W effective radiated power (1 kW equivalent isotropically radiated power) without the authorization otherwise required. The transmitting antenna elevation angle between the lower half-power (−3 dB relative to the peak or antenna bore sight) point and the horizon must always be greater than 10°.

(g) No station may transmit with a transmitter power exceeding 50 W PEP on the 33 cm band from within 241 km of the boundaries of the White Sands Missile Range. Its boundaries are those portions of Texas and New Mexico bounded on the south by latitude 31°41′ North, on the east by longitude 104°11′ West, on the north by latitude 34°30′ North, and on the west by longitude 107°30′ West.

(h) No station may transmit with a transmitter power exceeding 50 W PEP on the 219-220 MHz segment of the 1.25 m band.

(i) No station may transmit with an effective radiated power (ERP) exceeding 100 W PEP on the 60 m band. For the purpose of computing ERP, the transmitter PEP will be multiplied by the antenna gain relative to a half-wave dipole antenna. A half-wave dipole antenna will be presumed to have a gain of 1 (0 dBd). Licensees using other antennas must maintain in their station records either the antenna manufacturer's data on the antenna gain or calculations of the antenna gain.

(j) No station may transmit with a transmitter output exceeding 10 W PEP when the station is transmitting a SS emission type.

[54 FR 25857, June 20, 1989, as amended at 56 FR 37161, Aug. 5, 1991; 56 FR 3043, Jan. 28, 1991; 60 FR 15688, Mar. 27, 1995; 65 FR 6550, Feb. 10, 2000; 71 FR 66465, Nov. 15, 2006; 75 FR 27204, May 14, 2010; 75 FR 78171, Dec. 15, 2010; 76 FR 17569, Mar. 30, 2011; 77 FR 5413, Feb. 3, 2012]

## §97.315 Certification of external RF power amplifiers.

(a) Any external RF power amplifier (see §2.815 of the FCC Rules) manufactured or imported for use at an amateur radio station must be certificated for use in the amateur service in accordance with subpart J of part 2 of the FCC Rules. No amplifier capable of operation below 144 MHz may be constructed or modified by a non-amateur service licensee without a grant of certification from the FCC.

(b) The requirement of paragraph (a) does not apply if one or more of the following conditions are met:

(1) The amplifier is constructed or modified by an amateur radio operator for use at an amateur station.

(2) The amplifier was manufactured before April 28, 1978, and has been issued a marketing waiver by the FCC, or the amplifier was purchased before April 28, 1978, by an amateur radio operator for use at that operator's station.

(3) The amplifier is sold to an amateur radio operator or to a dealer, the amplifier is purchased in used condition by a dealer, or the amplifier is sold to an amateur radio operator for use at that operator's station.

(c) Any external RF power amplifier appearing in the Commission's database as certificated for use in the amateur service may be marketed for use in the amateur service.

[71 FR 66465, Nov. 15, 2006]

## §97.317 Standards for certification of external RF power amplifiers.

(a) To receive a grant of certification, the amplifier must:

(1) Satisfy the spurious emission standards of §97.307 (d) or (e) of this part, as applicable, when the amplifier is operated at the lesser of 1.5 kW PEP or its full output power and when the amplifier is placed in the "standby" or "off" positions while connected to the transmitter.

(2) Not be capable of amplifying the input RF power (driving signal) by more than 15 dB gain. Gain is defined as the ratio of the input RF power to the output RF power of the amplifier where both power measurements are expressed in peak envelope power or mean power.

(3) Exhibit no amplification (0 dB gain) between 26 MHz and 28 MHz.

(b) Certification shall be denied when:

(1) The Commission determines the amplifier can be used in services other than the Amateur Radio Service, or

(2) The amplifier can be easily modified to operate on frequencies between 26 MHz and 28 MHz.

[71 FR 66465, Nov. 15, 2006]

## Subpart E—Providing Emergency Communications

### §97.401 Operation during a disaster.

A station in, or within 92.6 km (50 nautical miles) of, Alaska may transmit emissions J3E and R3E on the channel at 5.1675 MHz (assigned frequency 5.1689 MHz) for emergency communications. The channel must be shared with stations licensed in the Alaska-Private Fixed Service. The transmitter power must not exceed 150 W PEP. A station in, or within 92.6 km of, Alaska may transmit communications for tests and training drills necessary to ensure the establishment, operation, and maintenance of emergency communication systems.

[71 FR 66465, Nov. 15, 2006]

## §97.403 Safety of life and protection of property.

No provision of these rules prevents the use by an amateur station of any means of radio communication at its disposal to provide essential communication needs in connection with the immediate safety of human life and immediate protection of property when normal communication systems are not available.

### §97.405 Station in distress.

(a) No provision of these rules prevents the use by an amateur station in distress of any means at its disposal to attract attention, make known its condition and location, and obtain assistance.

(b) No provision of these rules prevents the use by a station, in the exceptional circumstances described in paragraph (a) of this section, of any means of radio communications at its disposal to assist a station in distress.

**§97.407 Radio amateur civil emergency service.**

(a) No station may transmit in RACES unless it is an FCC-licensed primary, club, or military recreation station and it is certified by a civil defense organization as registered with that organization. No person may be the control operator of an amateur station transmitting in RACES unless that person holds a FCC-issued amateur operator license and is certified by a civil defense organization as enrolled in that organization.

(b) The frequency bands and segments and emissions authorized to the control operator are available to stations transmitting communications in RACES on a shared basis with the amateur service. In the event of an emergency which necessitates invoking the President's War Emergency Powers under the provisions of section 706 of the Communications Act of 1934, as amended, 47 U.S.C. 606, amateur stations participating in RACES may only transmit on the frequency segments authorized pursuant to part 214 of this chapter.

(c) An amateur station registered with a civil defense organization may only communicate with the following stations upon authorization of the responsible civil defense official for the organization with which the amateur station is registered:

(1) An amateur station registered with the same or another civil defense organization; and

(2) A station in a service regulated by the FCC whenever such communication is authorized by the FCC.

(d) All communications transmitted in RACES must be specifically authorized by the civil defense organization for the area served. Only civil defense communications of the following types may be transmitted:

(1) Messages concerning impending or actual conditions jeopardizing the public safety, or affecting the national defense or security during periods of local, regional, or national civil emergencies;

(2) Messages directly concerning the immediate safety of life of individuals, the immediate protection of property, maintenance of law and order, alleviation of human suffering and need, and the combating of armed attack or sabotage;

(3) Messages directly concerning the accumulation and dissemination of public information or instructions to the civilian population essential to the activities of the civil defense organization or other authorized governmental or relief agencies; and

(4) Communications for RACES training drills and tests necessary to ensure the establishment and maintenance of orderly and efficient operation of the RACES as ordered by the responsible civil defense organization served. Such drills and tests may not exceed a total time of 1 hour per week. With the approval of the chief officer for emergency planning in the applicable State, Commonwealth, District or territory, however, such tests and drills may be conducted for a period not to exceed 72 hours no more than twice in any calendar year.

[75 FR 78171, Dec. 15, 2010]

# Subpart F—Qualifying Examination Systems

## §97.501 Qualifying for an amateur operator license.

Each applicant must pass an examination for a new amateur operator license grant and for each change in operator class. Each applicant for the class of operator license grant specified below must pass, or otherwise receive examination credit for, the following examination elements:

(a) Amateur Extra Class operator: Elements 2, 3, and 4;

(b) General Class operator: Elements 2 and 3;

(c) Technician Class operator: Element 2.

[65 FR 6550, Feb. 10, 2000, as amended at 72 FR 3082, Jan. 24, 2007]

*Amateur Radio Service, Part 97*

**§97.503 Element standards.**

A written examination must be such as to prove that the examinee possesses the operational and technical qualifications required to perform properly the duties of an amateur service licensee. Each written examination must be comprised of a question set as follows:

(a) Element 2: 35 questions concerning the privileges of a Technician Class operator license. The minimum passing score is 26 questions answered correctly.

(b) Element 3: 35 questions concerning the privileges of a General Class operator license. The minimum passing score is 26 questions answered correctly.

(c) Element 4: 50 questions concerning the privileges of an Amateur Extra Class operator license. The minimum passing score is 37 questions answered correctly.

[54 FR 25857, June 20, 1989, as amended at 61 FR 41019, Aug. 7, 1996; 65 FR 6550, Feb. 10, 2000; 72 FR 3082, Jan. 24, 2007]

## §97.505 Element credit.

(a) The administering VEs must give credit as specified below to an examinee holding any of the following license grants or license documents:

(1) An unexpired (or expired but within the grace period for renewal) FCC-granted Advanced Class operator license grant: Elements 2 and 3.

(2) An unexpired (or expired but within the grace period for renewal) FCC-granted General Class operator license grant: Elements 2 and 3.

(3) An unexpired (or expired but within the grace period for renewal) FCC-granted Technician or Technician Plus Class operator (including a Technician Class operator license granted before February 14, 1991) license grant: Element 2.

(4) An expired FCC-issued Technician Class operator license document granted before March 21, 1987; Element 3.

(5) A CSCE: Each element the CSCE indicates the examinee passed within the previous 365 days.

(b) No examination credit, except as herein provided, shall be allowed on the basis of holding or having held any other license grant or document.

[59 FR 54834, Nov. 2, 1994, as amended at 63 FR 68980, Dec. 14, 1998; 65 FR 6551, Feb. 10, 2000; 69 FR 24997, May 5, 2004; 72 FR 3082, Jan. 24, 2007]

## §97.507 Preparing an examination.

(a) Each telegraphy message and each written question set administered to an examinee must be prepared by a VE holding an Amateur Extra Class operator license. A telegraphy message or written question set may also be prepared for the following elements by a VE holding an operator license of the class indicated:

(1) Element 3: Advanced Class operator.

(2) Elements 1 and 2: Advanced or General Class operators.

(b) Each question set administered to an examinee must utilize questions taken from the applicable question pool.

(c) Each telegraphy message and each written question set administered to an examinee for an amateur operator license must be prepared, or obtained from a supplier, by the administering VEs according to instructions from the coordinating VEC.

(d) A telegraphy examination must consist of a message sent in the international Morse code at no less than the prescribed speed for a minimum of 5 minutes. The message must contain each required telegraphy character at least once. No message known to the examinee may be administered in a telegraphy examination. Each 5 letters of the alphabet must be counted as 1 word. Each numeral, punctuation mark and prosign must be counted as 2 letters of the alphabet.

[54 FR 25857, June 20, 1989, as amended at 58 FR 29126, May 19, 1993; 59 FR 54834, Nov. 2, 1994; 65 FR 6551, Feb. 10, 2000; 69 FR 24997, May 5, 2004]

## §97.509 Administering VE requirements.

(a) Each examination for an amateur operator license must be administered by a team of at least 3 VEs at an examination session coordinated by a VEC. The number of examinees at the session may be limited.

(b) Each administering VE must:

(1) Be accredited by the coordinating VEC;

(2) Be at least 18 years of age;

(3) Be a person who holds an amateur operator license of the class specified below:

(i) Amateur Extra, Advanced or General Class in order to administer a Technician Class operator license examination;

(ii) Amateur Extra or Advanced Class in order to administer a General Class operator license examination;

(iii) Amateur Extra Class in order to administer an Amateur Extra Class operator license examination.

(4) Not be a person whose grant of an amateur station license or amateur operator license has ever been revoked or suspended.

(c) Each administering VE must be present and observing the examinee throughout the entire examination. The administering VEs are responsible for the proper conduct and necessary supervision of each examination. The administering VEs must immediately terminate the examination upon failure of the examinee to comply with their instructions.

(d) No VE may administer an examination to his or her spouse, children, grandchildren, stepchildren, parents, grandparents, stepparents, brothers, sisters, stepbrothers, stepsisters, aunts, uncles, nieces, nephews, and in-laws.

(e) No VE may administer or certify any examination by fraudulent means or for monetary or other consideration including reimbursement in any amount in excess of that permitted. Violation of this provision may result in the revocation of the grant of the VE's amateur station license and the suspension of the grant of the VE's amateur operator license.

(f) No examination that has been compromised shall be administered to any examinee. Neither the same telegraphy message nor the same question set may be re-administered to the same examinee.

(g) Passing a telegraphy receiving examination is adequate proof of an examinee's ability to both send and receive telegraphy. The administering VEs, however, may also include a sending segment in a telegraphy examination.

(h) Upon completion of each examination element, the administering VEs must immediately grade the examinee's answers. The administering VEs are responsible for determining the correctness of the examinee's answers.

(i) When the examinee is credited for all examination elements required for the operator license sought, 3 VEs must certify that the examinee is qualified for the license grant and that the VEs have complied with these administering VE requirements. The certifying VEs are jointly and individually accountable for the proper administration of each examination element reported. The certifying VEs may delegate to other qualified VEs their authority, but not their accountability, to administer individual elements of an examination.

(j) When the examinee does not score a passing grade on an examination element, the administering VEs must return the application document to the examinee and inform the examinee of the grade.

(k) The administering VEs must accommodate an examinee whose physical disabilities require a special examination procedure. The administering VEs may require a physician's certification indicating the nature of the disability before determining which, if any, special procedures must be used.

(l) The administering VEs must issue a CSCE to an examinee who scores a passing grade on an examination element.

(m) After the administration of a successful examination for an amateur operator license, the administering VEs must submit the application document to the coordinating VEC according to the coordinating VEC's instructions.

[59 FR 54834, Nov. 2, 1994, as amended at 61 FR 9953, Mar. 12, 1996; 62 FR 17567, Apr. 10, 1997; 63 FR 68980, Dec. 14, 1998; 65 FR 6551, Feb. 10, 2000; 71 FR 66465, Nov. 15, 2006]

**§97.511 Examinee conduct.**

Each examinee must comply with the instructions given by the administering VEs.

[59 FR 54835, Nov. 2, 1994]

**§97.513 VE session manager requirements.**

(a) A VE session manager may be selected by the VE team for each examination session. The VE session manager must be accredited as a VE by the same VEC that coordinates the examination session. The VE session manager may serve concurrently as an administering VE.

(b) The VE session manager may carry on liaison between the VE team and the coordinating VEC.

(c) The VE session manager may organize activities at an examination session.

[62 FR 17567, Apr. 10, 1997]

**§§97.515-97.517 [Reserved]**

## §97.519 Coordinating examination sessions.

(a) A VEC must coordinate the efforts of VEs in preparing and administering examinations.

(b) At the completion of each examination session, the coordinating VEC must collect applicant information and test results from the administering VEs. The coordinating VEC must:

(1) Screen collected information;

(2) Resolve all discrepancies and verify that the VE's certifications are properly completed; and

(3) For qualified examinees, forward electronically all required data to the FCC. All data forwarded must be retained for at least 15 months and must be made available to the FCC upon request.

(c) Each VEC must make any examination records available to the FCC, upon request

(d) The FCC may:

(1) Administer any examination element itself;

(2) Readminister any examination element previously administered by VEs, either itself or under the supervision of a VEC or VEs designated by the FCC; or

(3) Cancel the operator/primary station license of any licensee who fails to appear for readministration of an examination when directed by the FCC, or who does not successfully complete any required element that is readministered. In an instance of such cancellation, the person will be granted an operator/primary station license

consistent with completed examination elements that have not been invalidated by not appearing for, or by failing, the examination upon readministration.

[54 FR 25857, June 20, 1989, as amended at 59 FR 54835, Nov. 2, 1994; 62 FR 17567, Apr. 10, 1997; 63 FR 68981, Dec. 14, 1998; 71 FR 66465, Nov. 15, 2006]

## §97.521 VEC qualifications.

No organization may serve as a VEC unless it has entered into a written agreement with the FCC. The VEC must abide by the terms of the agreement. In order to be eligible to be a VEC, the entity must:

(a) Be an organization that exists for the purpose of furthering the amateur service;

(b) Be capable of serving as a VEC in at least the VEC region (see appendix 2) proposed;

(c) Agree to coordinate examinations for any class of amateur operator license;

(d) Agree to assure that, for any examination, every examinee qualified under these rules is registered without regard to race, sex, religion, national origin or membership (or lack thereof) in any amateur service organization;

[54 FR 25857, June 20, 1989, as amended at 58 FR 29127, May 19, 1993; 61 FR 9953, Mar. 12, 1996]

**§97.523 Question pools.**

All VECs must cooperate in maintaining one question pool for each written examination element. Each question pool must contain at least 10 times the number of questions required for a single examination. Each question pool must be published and made available to the public prior to its use for making a question set. Each question on each VEC question pool must be prepared by a VE holding the required FCC-issued operator license. See §97.507(a) of this part.

## 97.525 Accrediting VEs.

(a) No VEC may accredit a person as a VE if:

(1) The person does not meet minimum VE statutory qualifications or minimum qualifications as prescribed by this part;

(2) The FCC does not accept the voluntary and uncompensated services of the person;

(3) The VEC determines that the person is not competent to perform the VE functions; or

(4) The VEC determines that questions of the person's integrity or honesty could compromise the examinations.

(b) Each VEC must seek a broad representation of amateur operators to be VEs. No VEC may discriminate in accrediting VEs on the basis of race, sex, religion or national origin; nor on the basis of membership (or lack thereof) in an amateur service organization; nor on the basis of the person accepting or declining to accept reimbursement.

**§97.527 Reimbursement for expenses.**

VEs and VECs may be reimbursed by examinees for out-of-pocket expenses incurred in preparing, processing, administering, or coordinating an examination for an amateur operator license.

[66 FR 20752, Apr. 25, 2001]

**Appendix 1 to Part 97—Places Where the Amateur Service is Regulated by the FCC**

In ITU Region 2, the amateur service is regulated by the FCC within the territorial limits of the 50 United States, District of Columbia, Caribbean Insular areas [Commonwealth of Puerto Rico, United States Virgin Islands (50 islets and cays) and Navassa Island], and Johnston Island (Islets East, Johnston, North and Sand) and Midway Island (Islets Eastern and Sand) in the Pacific Insular areas.

In ITU Region 3, the amateur service is regulated by the FCC within the Pacific Insular territorial limits of American Samoa (seven islands), Baker Island, Commonwealth of Northern Mariana Islands, Guam Island, Howland Island, Jarvis Island, Kingman Reef, Palmyra Island (more than 50 islets) and Wake Island (Islets Peale, Wake and Wilkes).

## Appendix 2 to Part 97—VEC Regions

1. Connecticut, Maine, Massachusetts, New Hampshire, Rhode Island and Vermont.

2. New Jersey and New York.

3. Delaware, District of Columbia, Maryland and Pennsylvania.

4. Alabama, Florida, Georgia, Kentucky, North Carolina, South Carolina, Tennessee and Virginia.

5. Arkansas, Louisiana, Mississippi, New Mexico, Oklahoma and Texas.

6. California.

7. Arizona, Idaho, Montana, Nevada, Oregon, Utah, Washington and Wyoming.

8. Michigan, Ohio and West Virginia.

9. Illinois, Indiana and Wisconsin.

10. Colorado, Iowa, Kansas, Minnesota, Missouri, Nebraska, North Dakota and South Dakota.

11. Alaska.

12. Caribbean Insular areas.

13. Hawaii and Pacific Insular areas.

# Reference:

http://www.ecfr.gov/cgi-bin/text-idx?SID=08e0eedb66c207cc0980be258cf48308&node=47:5.0.1.1.6&rgn=div5

www.ingramcontent.com/pod-product-compliance
Lightning Source LLC
Chambersburg PA
CBHW051715170526
45167CB00002B/672